Women in the
Third World

Resource Directories previously published

Third World Resource Directory
Asia and Pacific
Latin America and Caribbean
Food, Hunger, Agribusiness

Women in the Third World

A Directory of Resources

Compiled and edited by

Thomas P. Fenton

and

Mary J. Heffron

ORBIS BOOKS

Maryknoll, New York 10545

Dedicated to the women of Africa, Asia and the Pacific, Latin America and the Caribbean, and the Middle East who have asked, with Filipina poet Marra Lanot:

> *Could it be possible*
> *It is wrong*
> *To stand and wait*
> *Like this. . .*
> *As my foremothers*
> *Did before me. . .*
> *Could it be possible*
> *It is wrong?*
> *Could it be*
> *Possible?*

The Catholic Foreign Mission Society of America (Maryknoll) recruits and trains people for overseas missionary service. Through Orbis Books Maryknoll aims to foster the international dialogue that is essential to mission. The books published, however, reflect the opinions of their authors and are not meant to represent the official position of the society.

Graphic Credits: *Alternative Trading News,* 49; CPF, 19; ISIS, 15, 66, 102; *Listen Real Loud,* 113; Lynn Roberson, Science for the People/CPF, 97; Rachel Burger/ CPF, 53, 119; Rini Templeton/dcgc, 68, 101; *Sojourners*/CPF, 70; *Who Owes Whom?*/Project Abraço, 54. All from Data Center Graphics (dcgc).

Published in the United States of America by Orbis Books, Maryknoll, NY 10545
Manufactured in the United States of America

ISBN 0-88344-530-1

Contents

Chapter 1: Organizations   *1*

Annotated Entries   1
Organization name; address; telephone number; organization's self-description; keyword descriptions of the organization's political and religious affiliation, region and issue focus, activities, and resources; and title of periodical publications.
Supplementary List of Organizations   15
Information Sources   19

Chapter 2: Books   *21*

Annotated Entries   21
Author(s) or editor(s); title; place of publication; publisher; date of publication; number of pages; price; keyword description of format; description of content.
    General   21
    Bibliographies   41
    Catalogs, Directories, Guides   44
    Study Guides and Curriculum Materials   45
    Reference Books   48
Supplementary List of Books   50
Information Sources   53

Chapter 3: Periodicals   *55*

Annotated Entries   55
Title; publisher; address; number of issues per year; format (newspaper, magazine, or newsletter); size (height in centimeters); number of pages; subscription costs; keyword description of format; description of content.
Supplementary List of Periodicals   66
Information Sources   68

Foreword

Are women in Africa, Asia, and Latin America organizing as women? Is there a global women's movement? How can we support the struggles of women in other countries?

These are questions we are frequently asked, particularly by North Americans, writing or visiting us at the Isis International resource centers in Rome, Italy, or Santiago, Chile.

The best response we can give is to direct them to the wealth of resources — publications, documents, audiovisuals — that women are producing as part of their organizing efforts all over the world.

Most people are simply amazed: "We had no idea the women's movement was so strong in the Third World! Why there is a real hidden treasure of materials out there!"

Hidden, but not purposely. Women's groups in the Third World simply do not have the means to make the resources they produce more widely known. That is why *Women in the Third World: A Directory of Resources* is so welcome. With its annotated listings of printed and audiovisual materials by and about women in Africa, Asia and the Pacific, Latin America and the Caribbean, and the Middle East, this directory opens the door to these richly varied resources.

Women all over the world, from very diverse countries, backgrounds, and cultural contexts, are claiming the space to tell their own stories, define their own issues, create their own organizations, and build their own networks. The growing women's movement, especially in the Third World, is bringing new and creative perspectives to crucial issues from the debt crisis to sexual violence, from militarism to reproductive rights, from union organizing to domestic work and family life, from racism to the impact of new technology on our lives. The women's movement is challenging views often firmly held even among progressives and alternative groups and is bringing new insights to what it means to work for a more just society.

Leafing through the pages of this directory gives a feeling for the breadth, depth, and dynamism of women's consciousness-raising and organizational efforts in the Third World. Here are the voices of Central American women, suffering in strife-torn situations, of women from rural villages in Asia drawn by poverty into the sex-tourism industry in the capital cities or around U.S. military bases, of Mexican women working in U.S.-owned border industries, or Third World women explaining just what the world economic crisis means to the survival chances of millions of families like their own.

Many lessons can be learned by listening to these voices. Lessons that can help those people and groups in the West who are concerned about building understanding, cooperation, and links of solidarity with other peoples around the world.

The strength and dynamism of the women's movement in the Third World was evident at the forum of Non-Governmental Organizations (NGO) in Nairobi, Kenya in July 1985. More than 13,000 women from all over the world gathered there, not for formal plenary sessions and resolutions, but for hundreds of workshops, discussions, film, video, and slide showings, cultural presentations, exhibits, and demonstrations. A significant difference with previous Women's Decade NGO events (Mexico City, 1975; Copenhagen, 1980) was the predominance of women's voices from the Third World. The forum showed the great growth that had taken place from 1975 to 1985 in the awareness of and respect for both the similarities and the differences in the situation of women from so many countries and backgrounds.

Grounded in mutual understanding and respect, these women, who represented only the tip of the iceberg, came to Nairobi prepared to work out ways of going forward, cooperating as much as possible, for the empowerment of the most oppressed women that they might participate in a better world.

What made this all possible? The growing strength of women's groups and organizations in the Third World, for one thing. Information and communication for another.

Excluded from the mainstream media, the women's movement has created its own. Not finding the existing communications channels responsive to or useful for their needs, women have built their own channels and networks for sharing ideas and experiences, for communicating and learning from each other.

The women's movement has long recognized the power of information and the importance of communication and networking. This is evident from the impressive array of women's organizations, media, resource centers, and networks you will find described in this directory. Many of these organizations were created and continue to operate with few financial or material resources. Few of them have the time, energy, or money to publicize their existence. Consequently their potential is not fully realized: the voices and perspectives of women in the Third World are not being heard as widely as they should be, neither in the West nor in the Third World itself. Indeed, many in the Third World who might join forces with these groups or make use of their resources do not know of their existence.

In its work of fostering communication among women around the world, Isis International is confronted daily with the problem of how to spread the word about existing women's groups, networks, and resources. We very much appreciate the efforts that Mary Heffron and Tom Fenton have put into compiling this directory of resources; it is an important contribution to making these women's groups, organizations, networks, resource centers, media, and materials more widely known. This directory will be very useful in both the West and in the Third World to people seeking to join with others for action and solidarity.

Making the global connections with women's struggles in the Third World will strengthen all of our work and struggles everywhere.

MARILEE KARL, COORDINATOR
ISIS INTERNATIONAL
(ROME AND SANTIAGO)

Preface

This directory of resources on women in the Third World is one in a series of twelve volumes on Third World regions and issues that is being compiled by the Data Center's Third World Resources project.

OBJECTIVES

Our aim in compiling this and all the other resource guides in the twelve-volume series is to meet five objectives:

1. To strengthen the ties among organizations that oppose the injustices in foreign military and economic intervention in the Third World by helping to dismantle the institutional, issue-related, and regional barriers that now divide these groups.

Educators and activists who take a critical stance toward the impact of foreign intervention in Third World affairs are unnecessarily divided from one another and thus not as effective or as mutually supportive as they could be. They are divided institutionally, by issue orientation, and by region.

Institutional walls separate church workers from academics, community organizers from researchers, and social studies teachers from political activists. Third World Resources seeks to breach these institutional walls by publicizing the work of groups in all of these categories and by promoting their resources through a worldwide network of Third World–related progressive organizations.

Ironically, *issues* also drive wedges among activist organizations. Nuclear groups work on freeze issues, but fail to appreciate fully the urgency of the work of Central America–support organizations and vice versa. While this might make some sense tactically and while this focus of energies is perfectly understandable given the demands on the time of organizers, the lack of a network of mutually supportive progressive organizations clearly limits the impact of their work.

By putting people in touch with people — whatever the issue that may be their prime concern, Third World Resources encourages better cross-fertilization of ideas and plans. This results in more effective joint action and less duplication of effort in the production of education and action resources.

Regional barriers also fragment the resistance movement. Transnational corporations are — unfortunately — years ahead of their critics in realizing the need to have near-instantaneous communication across regional and national boundaries. Critics need to appreciate as well the importance of the broadest and quickest possible interchange of information and of plans for action.

Third World Resources transcends regional boundaries by including in this directory and in all its publications education- and action-oriented resources from all over the world. In this international aspect of our work we are helped by an international board of advisors and by our affiliation with Interdoc, an international network of research and documentation centers.

2. To legitimize and give equal time to alternative points of view on Third World affairs in general and on the involvement of the United States and other major powers in the Third World in particular.

In the United States critical analyses of the devastating impact of foreign public and private interests in the Third World are woefully underrepresented on library shelves across the country, and the challenging voice of oppressed Third World peoples is heard only as a whisper in the media and in classrooms. We suspect that this criticism applies equally well to other major industrialized powers.

— Yet analytical and educational work of this nature *is* being done. The array of resources presented in this directory testifies to that fact. This work *must* be publicized more widely.

— Critical Third World voices *are* crying out for justice. These voices *must* be magnified.

Commenting on the *Third World Resource Directory* (Orbis Books, 1984) the director of the Third World Studies Center in Manila has said: "The publication of the resource directory is truly heartwarming, for it tells us abundantly that in America not everyone has been silent or silenced and that many are laboring to explain the links between the behavior of the U.S. government and multinationals and the problems that we face in our own countries."

The purpose of the present directory is to publicize the efforts of those who are explaining these links and to make certain that the victims of interventionism by the United States and other powers have an opportunity to tell their story.

3. To promote the education/action resources of Third World-related organizations in a sustained, focused, and professional manner.

Data Center president Fred Goff described this problem in his Foreword to the *Third World Resource Directory:* "All too often the limited resources available to these [progressive] organizations are consumed by the process of producing a given book, pamphlet, newsletter, or film. Little energy or money remains for adequately publicizing these resources."

Anyone who has worked in solidarity and anti-intervention organizations knows how true this observation is. Even when the desire is there to reach beyond the institutional, issue-related, and regional barriers described above, the energy and financial resources that this outreach demands is too often just not there. This results in the under-utilization of available resources and—perhaps even worse—the waste of limited time and money in the production of redundant resources.

Third World Resources furthers the promotional outreach of progressive organizations by focusing its energies on *identifying* and *acquiring* resources from all over the world on regions such as Asia and the Pacific and on issues such as human rights, on *describing* and *evaluating* the resources in a careful, non-rhetorical fashion, on *presenting* them in an attractive, readily accessible format, and on *publicizing* the work of these organizations to a broad audience of educators, researchers, librarians, and political activists.

4. To put in the hands of researchers and organizers in the Third World comprehensive guides to Third World–related organizations and educational resources in other parts of the world.

Data Center president Fred Goff spoke to this problem as well: "Researchers and organizers in the Third World have learned from experience that information critical to their struggle for social justice—information about the realities of power in their own countries—is often available only here in the United States" (Foreword, *Third World Resource Directory*).

Third World Resources responds to this need of activists and educators in the Third World by providing them with handy sourcebooks of annotated descriptions and comprehensive lists of organizations, books, magazines, films, and other resources on a wide variety of Third World regions and related issues. The *Third World Resources* newsletter keeps these references current, and the Third World Resources documentation clearinghouse at the Data Center assures easy access to the entire collection of resources from anywhere in the world.

5. To direct concerned citizens in First World countries to the books, periodicals, audiovisuals, and other resources they need to study in order to take informed and effective action to correct injustices in the ways their governments and businesses treat Third World nations and peoples.

This directory and the others in the twelve-volume set are designed to offer immediate answers to the questions concerned citizens ask: How can I find out more about the impact of transnational corporations in Southeast Asia? What can I read to help me understand what is happening in the Middle East? What steps can I take to help people in the Philippines or to stop U.S. intervention in Central America? Where can I rent a good educational film on South Africa?

THIRD WORLD RESOURCES

The present directory and the entire twelve-volume set of resource directories update and expand the resources presented in the *Third*

World Resource Directory (Orbis Books, 1984) and complement the two other facets of Third World Resources: a quarterly newsletter and resource guide and a clearinghouse of Third World-related resources.

Quarterly Newsletter and Resource Guide

Third World Resources publishes a sixteen-page quarterly newsletter, *Third World Resources: A Quarterly Review of Resources from and about the Third World,* with notices and descriptive listings of organizations and newly released print, audiovisual, and other educational resources from and about the Third World. Each issue of the newsletter contains a unique four-page resource guide that provides comprehensive coverage of one particular region or issue. This resource guide is available at discounts for bulk distribution.

Clearinghouse of Third World–related Resources

In order to insure the widest possible access to the resources gathered in the course of work on the resource directories and newsletter Third World Resources catalogs and integrates all incoming information and materials into the library collection of the Data Center where they can be used by the hundreds of journalists, teachers, community organizers, and others who visit the center's public-access library each year. The materials are also avaiable to the center's national and international network of Search Service clients.

In addition, bibliographical data on all of the resources are stored in a computerized data base to facilitate identification and retrieval of cross-referenced resources and to pave the way for future on-line access to this unique storehouse of critical information.

APPRECIATION

The work of Third World Resources is sustained by friends all over the world who give generously of their time, money, resources, kind words, and encouragement. This directory and all our efforts are dedicated to them with heartfelt thanks for their support.

We thank all at Orbis Books, especially John Eagleson and the late Philip Scharper for encouraging us to produce this series of books and Hank Schlau for his careful and thorough editing. Our thanks also go to the Maryknoll Fathers and Brothers for a grant in support of our work.

We acknowledge in a special way the assistance of the Data Center and of the hard-working and underpaid staffs of two women's resource centers: Isis International (Rome and Santiago) and Peoples Translation Service (Oakland). We also thank the members of the Third World Resources Advisory Council.

Introduction

The table of contents (above) is a guide to the overall structure of this directory. Each of the five chapters opens with an introduction that describes the format and contents of the particular chapter.

In this introduction we offer comments on the format and content of the directory as a whole.

FORMAT

This directory updates and expands the resources in the chapter on women in the *Third World Resource Directory* (Orbis Books, 1984). That chapter (pp. 220–43), as well as cross-referenced entries throughout the 1984 directory, should be consulted for complementary annotated lists of organizations and their resources on women in the Third World.

We have tried to include complete descriptive and ordering information for every citation in this directory. Addresses for the organizations, publishers, and distributors appear either in the organizations index in the back of the book or with the actual entry. In some cases — such as in the periodicals chapter — we provided the address with the entry, for ease of ordering.

We caution you to inquire about current prices and terms of sale or rental before placing an order for any item in this directory.

CONTENT

Our comments on the content of this directory and of the resources themselves fall into three categories: definitions, scope, and political orientation.

Definitions

We use the term *Third World* in a geographical sense to encompass the people and countries of Africa, Asia and Pacific, Latin America and Caribbean, and the Middle East. In order to limit this directory to a modest size we have not focused on real and urgent concerns of women who live in "Third World" conditions in the industrialized nations of North America, Europe, and other areas. We refer you to the sources of information in each of the chapters of this directory for indirect references to resources on those issues.

Scope

In compiling this directory we endeavored to identify and acquire resources on women in the Third World from organizations in all parts of the world. We acknowledge, however, that we still have a long way to go toward our goal of making the resources truly international in origin.

We realize that we have probably overlooked significant organizations and resources and that certain issues and regions have not been given the attention they deserve. We ask that you take into account the severe limits of time, funds, and geographical location within which we work and that you work with us to expand the reach of future editions of this directory.

Organizations were selected for inclusion in this directory because their work is predominantly focused on women. Concerns about the size of this directory forced us to omit organizations whose focus is much broader than that one issue. No directory on women in the Third World would be complete without the education and action resources of organizations whose work is international or global in scope or whose focus of concern is only indirectly related to women. We urge you to consult the references given in the information sources section of each chapter for the names and addresses of complementary organizations such as these. See also the other directories in this twelve-volume set, all of which will contain resources on women.

Political Orientation

In the preface to the *Third World Resource Directory* we described the resources in that directory as — by and large — "partisan and biased" in favor of a "radical analysis" of Third World affairs. We described this radical analysis as one that contends that:

• reforms in the system are not enough; the crying need is for radical (that is, fundamental) changes in economic, political, and social (race, sex, and class) relations;

• change will come about through struggles (though not necessarily violent ones) between the "powerful" and the "powerless";

• the private and public institutional power of countries like the United States is often used to frustrate initiatives for fundamental social change in Third World countries.

Even a cursory examination of educational resources about the Third World clearly demonstrates that most resources — and certainly the bulk of what we are exposed to in the media—ignore this "radical" analysis in favor of one that:

- stresses reforms that do not upset the present disposition of power;
- characterizes all people in the First World countries as rich and powerful and describes all in the Third World as poor and powerless;
- judges all struggles for radical social change to be Soviet-inspired and, therefore, to be opposed.

We situate the issue of women in the Third World in this "radical" political context. The resources we have selected for inclusion in this directory reflect the thinking of women (and men) who have come to the conclusion that the development of women in the Third World demands *fundamental* changes in the status quo.

While openly admitting our political orientation we feel it is also important to point out that political biases are woven into most—if not all—education and action resources on the regions and issues we are covering—whether those resources be left-wing, right-wing, or moderate in character. One cannot describe or analyze events in the Third World without betraying the lines of a political belief system regarding the means and pace of social change, the causes of social unrest, the allegiance owed one's own government, and so forth.

We have been straightforward about our own partisanship because we believe strongly that it is important for all to identify, evaluate, and admit to the biases that inform their analysis of and decisions regarding Third World affairs. Educators and librarians especially should be diligent about calling attention to the political biases in *all* of the resources on their desks and shelves—not just those that are alternative or radical in orientation.

In compiling a directory of alternative resources we are not advocating the wholesale substitution of one body of thought for another. For one thing, as a careful study of the resources in this directory will demonstrate, there is no "one body of thought" on the varied and numerous issues treated below—even though many of the resources could be labeled as alternative and politically radical. For another, a confession of one's political biases is not necessarily to be equated with a lack of appreciation for or openness to the truth in other points of view.

Our overriding aim is to promote the critical and responsible study of the alternative points of view represented in the resources in this directory along with consideration of all other descriptions and analyses of Third World affairs.

1

Organizations

This chapter is divided into three parts: annotated entries, supplementary list of organizations, and sources of additional information.

Each **annotated entry** includes: organization name; address; telephone number; organization's self-description (in quotation marks); keyword descriptions of the organization's political and religious affiliation, focus (first geographical, then according to issues), activities, and resources; and title(s) of periodical(s).

The keywords were selected by the organizations themselves and are intended to provide a quick overview of each organization's work. The descriptors are neither all-inclusive nor scientific.

If the name of a periodical stands alone, this means that the magazine, newsletter, or newspaper is fully annotated in the periodicals chapter below. Otherwise, pertinent descriptive information accompanies the citation.

Organizations in the **supplementary list** (pp. 15–19) are grouped under these headings: Africa; Asia and Pacific; Europe; Latin America and Caribbean; Middle East; and North America. Entries in this section include the organization's name and address.

The **information sources** section (pp. 19–20) provides the titles of directories and guides that contain the names of other organizations related to women in the Third World.

All of the organizations and periodicals in this chapter are listed in the appropriate indexes at the back of this directory.

ANNOTATED ENTRIES

American Friends Service Committee, Nationwide Women's Program, 1501 Cherry St., Philadelphia, PA 19102. Tel: (215) 241-7160.

"AFSC's Nationwide Women's Program works to promote communication about women among regional, national, and overseas staff, com-

1

mittee members, and others within the AFSC orbit. Through its quarterly newsletter the NWP does outreach to individuals and groups in the women's movement and other movements with whom we share solidarity and issue priorities."

RELIGIOUS AFFILIATION: Religious Society of Friends.

FOCUS: Third World general. Women • labor • political economy • transnational corporations • refugees • reproductive rights.

ACTIVITIES: Popular education • political action • workshops and seminars • overseas project support • justice and peace ministries • program development and resourcing within AFSC network.

RESOURCES: Speakers • audiovisuals • books and literature • reports.

PERIODICAL: *Listen Real Loud.*

AMES: Salvadoran Women's Association, P.O. Box 40311, San Francisco, CA 94140. Tel: (415) 552-5015. Inquire for addresses of regional offices elsewhere in the United States and in Nicaragua, Costa Rica, France, Canada, and Mexico.

"AMES, the Association of Salvadoran Women, is a voice, a tool, a collective means through which Salvadoran women can work for the equality and justice currently lacking [in El Salvador]. Since our founding in 1979, over ten thousand Salvadoran women have joined AMES: homemakers, peasants, students, professionals, laborers, market women, and refugees. We provide Salvadoran women with the skills they need to participate in community projects and decisions. By necessity, our advocacy must currently focus on securing the basics of survival—drinking water, food, housing, medical care, fair wages. Ultimately, we seek to transform El Salvador into a society which honors human rights, women's equality, and the well-being of its children."

FOCUS: El Salvador • Nicaragua. Women • national liberation struggles • food, hunger, agribusiness • education • health • children • refugees.

ACTIVITIES: Overseas project support • popular education • solidarity work • networking • distribution of print matter • distribution of audiovisuals • fundraising.

RESOURCES: Speakers • audiovisuals • consultant services.

Center for Women's Resources, 43 Roces Ave., Mar Santos Bldg., 2nd floor, Quezon City, Philippines. Tel: 78-79-41.

"A service bureau active in providing information on the situation of women in the Philippines, developing educational modules for groups and institutions, conducting research on women's concerns, linking women's groups in the country and building contacts with women around the world, and supporting women's campaigns for equality and emancipation."

FOCUS: Asia and Pacific. Human rights • women • transnational corporations • population control • tourism and prostitution.

ACTIVITIES: Research and writing • political action • networking •

documentation and dissemination of information • workshops and seminars • training.

RESOURCES: Research services • books and literature • library.

Church Women United, 475 Riverside Dr., Rm. 812, New York, NY 10115. Tel: (212) 870-2344; and 777 UN Plaza, New York, NY 10017. Tel: (212) 661-3856.

"A national movement of Protestant, Roman Catholic, Orthodox, and other Christian women."

RELIGIOUS AFFILIATION: Ecumenical.

FOCUS: Global. Human rights • militarism, peace, disarmament • transnational corporations • social justice • food, hunger, agribusiness • corporate responsibility.

ACTIVITIES: Political action • solidarity work • networking • constituency education • legislative action • overseas project support.

RESOURCES: Speakers • study-action guides • consultant services • legislative alerts.

PERIODICAL: *The Church Woman. lead time.* 4 issues/year. Membership newsletter.

Coalition for Women in International Development, c/o OEF International, 2101 L St., NW, Suite 916, Washington, DC 20037. Tel: (202) 466-3430.

"Established in 1976, the coalition is composed of leaders and representatives of national organizations—professional, church related, and community—and women who participate as individuals in pursuit of the following goals: (1) Inform and influence U.S. policy makers about issues affecting women and their families in the developing world; and (2) Mobilize support throughout the United States for policies that recognize women as partners in both the work and the benefits of development."

POLITICAL AFFILIATION: Bipartisan.

FOCUS: Global. Women • development.

ACTIVITIES: Popular education • networking • constituency education • legislative action • Congressional testimony • conferences • off-the-record briefings.

Committee for Asian Women, 57 Peking Rd., 5/F, Kowloon, Hongkong. Tel: (3) 682187.

"CAW aims to assist local women workers groups in consciousness-raising and effect changes to overcome the oppressive situation of women workers in Asia—both as women and as workers. CAW works through educational seminars and programmes on the local, sub-regional, and regional levels."

RELIGIOUS AFFILIATION: Joint ecumenical program of the Christian Conference of Asia–Urban Rural Mission and the Office for Human Development of the Federation of Asian Bishops Conference.

FOCUS: Asia and Pacific. Women • labor • transnational corporations • social justice.

ACTIVITIES: Popular education • research and writing • networking • documentation and dissemination of information • workshops and seminars • overseas project support.
RESOURCES: Audiovisuals • books and literature.
PERIODICAL: *Asian Women Workers Newsletter*. 4 issues/year.

Institute for Policy Studies, Third World Women's Project, 1901 Q St., NW, Washington, DC 20009. Tel: (202) 234–9382.

"The Third World Women's Project sponsors tours of Third World women who are active in socio-economic justice struggles and women's issues in their countries to speak across the United States and Europe. The speakers meet with community, church, women's, and university groups to dialogue about Third World issues, particularly those concerning women."

FOCUS: Third World general • Latin America and Caribbean • Africa • Asia and Pacific. Human rights • militarism, peace, disarmament • foreign aid and trade • labor • political economy • international awareness • national liberation struggles • transnational corporations • social justice • native peoples • food, hunger, agribusiness • cultural recuperation.
ACTIVITIES: Popular education • political action • research and writing • intern programs • media relations • networking • film and slideshow production • constituency education • policy-oriented research and writing • documentation and dissemination of information • distribution of print matter • distribution of audiovisuals • workshops and seminars • tours of Third World women in the United States and Europe.
RESOURCES: Speakers • audiovisuals • curriculum guides • books and literature • resource center on Third World women.

Institute for Women's Studies in the Arab World, Beirut University College, P.O. Box 13–5053, Beirut, Lebanon. Tel: 811968.

"With a grant from the Ford Foundation, Beirut University College, long a leader in women's education in the Middle East, established the Institute for Women's Studies in the Arab World in October 1973. The institute encourages and evaluates research into the history, condition, and evolving needs of women in the Arab world. Based on this research, the institute engages in action programs to educate and assist the contemporary Arab woman, and in communications programs to transmit, regionally and internationally, a better understanding of the Arab woman—her traditional role, her place in today's society, and her aspirations and potential for the future."

FOCUS: Arab world. Women • labor • education • child development • legal and social status of women • rural development • contemporary Arab literature • career development.
ACTIVITIES: Research and writing • intern programs • documentation and dissemination of information • library services • workshops, seminars, conferences • publisher • teacher training.

RESOURCES: Library • books and monographs • consultant services • research papers (unpublished) • research services.

PERIODICAL: *Al Raida.* 4 issues/year. Newsletter.

Institute of Social Studies Trust, Women's Studies Programme, 5 Deen Dayal Upadhyay Marg, SMM Theatre Crafts Bldg., New Delhi 110002, India. Tel: 331-2972.

"The institute works in several areas such as data collection, research, and analysis: as an intermediary organisation which influences policy-making and planning bodies; as a social action and service organisation; and, lastly, as a documentation and dissemination of information storage, retrieval, and dissemination centre."

FOCUS: Third World general. Women • labor • social justice.

ACTIVITIES: Research and writing • intern programs • networking • documentation and dissemination of information • technical and organizational assistance.

RESOURCES: Research services • books and literature • consultant services • library • reports.

International Center for Research on Women, 1010 16 St., NW, 3rd floor, Washington, DC 20036. Tel: (202) 293-3154.

"ICRW focuses on women's work in the Third World and strategies to expand their economic opportunities through research, technical assistance, public education, and public information programs. Priorities include investigating critical aspects of women's economic roles, providing technical assistance to development agencies in the design and evaluation of employment and income-generation projects, and translating research findings into policy recommendations on behalf of women."

FOCUS: Third World general. Women • international development • income generation.

ACTIVITIES: Library services • popular education • intern programs • policy-oriented research and writing • workshops and seminars • technical assistance • policy round tables.

RESOURCES: Library • books and literature • working papers.

International Council of Women (ICW), 13 rue Caumartin, 75009 Paris, France. Tel: (331) 47 4219 40.

"ICW's principal objectives are: (1) To promote equal rights and responsibilities for both men and women in all spheres by removing all forms of discrimination based on birth, race, sex, language, or religion; (2) To support all efforts to achieve peace through negotiation, arbitration, and conciliation; and (3) To encourage the integration of women in development and in decision-making bodies."

FOCUS: Global. Human rights • militarism, peace, disarmament • food, hunger, agribusiness • transnational corporations • social welfare and family • education • health.

ACTIVITIES: Workshops and seminars • political action • networking • constituency education • project development with international agencies.

RESOURCES: Books and literature • reports • anthologies of women's poetry.

PERIODICAL: *ICW Newsletter.* 3 issues/year.

International Defense and Aid Fund for Southern Africa, Women's Committee, P.O. Box 17, Cambridge, MA 02238. Tel: (617) 491-8343.

"The 1980 world conference of the United Nations Decade for Women adopted a program of action which called for 'legal, humanitarian, moral, and political assistance to women inside South Africa and Namibia persecuted under repressive and discriminatory legislation and practices, to their families, and to women in refugee camps.' Women around the world are answering that call. In the United States the Women's Committee of IDAF was formed to organize a network among women for the support and assistance of black women in Southern Africa. We work through women's groups, churches, and clubs."

FOCUS: Southern Africa. Women • labor • apartheid • refugees.

ACTIVITIES: Popular education • solidarity work • networking • documentation and dissemination of information.

RESOURCES: Speakers • books and literature • consultant services.

International Research and Training Institute for the Advancement of Women (INSTRAW), Avenida César Nicolás Penson 102-A, P.O. Box 21747, Santo Domingo, Dominican Republic. Tel: (809) 685-2111.

"The primary objective of the institute's research, training, and information programme is to ensure that sustained attention is given to the integration of women into development activities at all levels. The Institute pursues this objective through research, training, information gathering, documentation, and communication activities."

POLITICAL AFFILIATION: United Nations.

FOCUS: Global. Women • labor • transnational corporations • food, hunger, agribusiness • development • health • energy • natural resources.

ACTIVITIES: Research and writing • networking • library services • documentation and dissemination of information • publishing • distribution of print matter • workshops and seminars • technical training.

RESOURCES: Research services • books and literature • consultant services • library.

PERIODICAL: *INSTRAW News.* 6 issues/year. Magazine.

International Women's Tribune Centre, 777 United Nations Plaza, New York, NY 10017. Tel: (212) 687-8633.

"The centre was founded in 1976 to respond to requests for information on development projects and the United Nations following the International Women's Year Tribune held in Mexico City (1975). The IWTC has since developed a resource centre, a number of publications and audiovisual materials, and other services aimed especially at women involved in international development projects."

FOCUS: Third World general. Women • development.

ACTIVITIES: Networking • library services • documentation and dis-

semination of information • workshops and seminars • technical assistance and training.
RESOURCES: Audiovisuals • books and literature • library.
PERIODICAL: *The Tribune. La Tribuna. La Tribune.*

International Women's Watch, 464 19 St., Oakland, CA 94612. Tel: (415) 835-9631.

"IWW is now in the process of gathering information about the types of work women do (with and without pay), how much say they have in the work they do, what kind of pay they receive, and the kinds of places where they work. IWW sponsored a forum at the United Nations conference in Nairobi (1985); the forum was concerned with how women's work affects national economies and the effect that transnational corporate policies have on women and their work."

RELIGIOUS AFFILIATION: Ecumenical.
FOCUS: Global • Africa • Asia and Pacific. Women • labor • political economy • international awareness • transnational corporations • native peoples • food, hunger, agribusiness • economic justice.
ACTIVITIES: Popular education • political action • networking • constituency education • legislative action • documentation and dissemination of information • workshops and seminars.
RESOURCES: Speakers.

Isis International, Via Santa Maria dell'Anima 30, 00186 Rome, Italy. Tel: (06) 6565842; and Casilla 2067, Correo Central, Santiago, Chile. Tel: 490271.

"Isis International draws on a network of over ten thousand contacts in 150 countries and a resource center with thousands of documents and publications from all over the world to provide information and communication services on a wide range of issues that concern women."

FOCUS: International. Women • development • health • transnational corporations • education • communication • migration and tourism.
ACTIVITIES: Media • solidarity work • networking • documentation and dissemination of information • publishing • workshops and seminars.
RESOURCES: Books and literature • consultant services • library • training and technical assistance.
PERIODICAL: *Isis International Women's Journal.* Supplement: *Women in Action.*

Isis-WICCE: Women's International Cross-Cultural Exchange, Case Postale 2471, CH-1211 Geneva 2, Switzerland. Tel: (022) 33 67 46.

"Isis-WICCE is a women's international resource centre that aims: (1) To improve women's situations through information exchange and direct exchange; (2) To promote ideas and actions that contribute to the eradication of injustice based on sex discrimination; and (3) To promote international information and communication networks designed to help women combat discrimination and injustice against them and to strengthen them in these actions. Each year the activities of Isis-WICCE are focused around a specific theme, such as communications, health, and technology."

FOCUS: Global. Women.

ACTIVITIES: Research and writing • intern programs • media relations • networking • policy-oriented research and writing • library services • press service • documentation and dissemination of information • publishing • workshops and seminars • foreign service • training and technical assistance • exchange program.

RESOURCES: Lending library • curriculum guides • books and literature • consultant services • bibliographies and documentation packets.

PERIODICAL: *Women's World.*

Kali for Women, N84 Panchshila Park, New Delhi 110017, India; and B26 Gulmohar Park, New Delhi 110049.

"Kali, a powerful and dynamic Hindu goddess, has been chosen as the name of an organization that seeks to increase the body of knowledge on women in the Third World. Equally the organization is concerned with ensuring that, as far as possible, Third World women be provided an opportunity — and a forum — to speak out for themselves, rather than have their situation represented, as it has hitherto been, by the West."

FOCUS: Third World general. Women • political economy • social justice • literacy • children.

ACTIVITIES: Publishing • popular education • political action • media relations • film and slideshow production • training women in printing • reprinting articles.

RESOURCES: Books and literature.

MADRE, c/o Women's Peace Network, 853 Broadway, New York, NY 10003.

"MADRE (Spanish for 'mother') is engaged in supplying direct aid to improve health care in Central America, particularly in Nicaragua where a horrible terrorist war is underway because the so-called contras, supported by the United States, are trying to overthrow the government."

FOCUS: Nicaragua. Women • health care • children.

ACTIVITIES: Overseas project support • popular education • networking.

RESOURCES: Speakers • consultant services.

Manushi, C1/202 Lajpat Nagar, New Delhi 110024, India. Tel: 617022.

"Manushi is an autonomous women's group which does not accept any institutional funding. We publish a bimonthly journal, *Manushi*, in English and Hindi, focusing on women's lives and struggles for change, especially in the Indian subcontinent. We also undertake research and organising actions around women's and civil rights issues and provide legal aid to women."

FOCUS: Third World general, particularly the Indian subcontinent. Women • human rights • social justice • food, hunger, agribusiness • civil rights.

ACTIVITIES: Research and writing • solidarity work • media relations • policy-oriented research and writing • publishing • legal aid to women • counseling.

RESOURCES: Speakers • books and literature.

PERIODICAL: *Manushi: A Journal about Women and Society.*

Match International Centre, 171 Nepean St., No. 401, Ottawa, Ontario K2P OB4 Canada. Tel: (613) 238–1312.

"Match International Centre is a unique Canadian development agency in that it is run by and for women. We take the view that international development is a women's issue and women's issues are development issues. Match's two main goals are to financially assist women's projects in developing countries and to educate the Canadian public about women and development."

FOCUS: Asia • Africa • Latin America and Caribbean. Women • labor • political economy • national liberation struggles • transnational corporations • social justice • native peoples • food, hunger, agribusiness.

ACTIVITIES: Popular education • research and writing • solidarity work • intern programs • media relations • networking • film and slideshow production • constituency education • policy-oriented research and writing • library services • documentation and dissemination of information • publishing • distribution of print matter • distribution of audiovisuals • workshops and seminars • overseas project support.

RESOURCES: Speakers • audiovisuals • study-action guides • books and literature • consultant services • library.

PERIODICAL: *Match Newsletter.*

Najda: Women Concerned about the Middle East, P.O. Box 7152, Berkeley, CA 94707.

"Launched in 1960 during the final stages of the Algerian war of independence, Najda (an Arabic word meaning 'assistance in time of need') continues today to provide medical and financial aid to the Arab world wherever the need is greatest. At the same time, Najda attempts to promote understanding between Arabs and North Americans by sponsoring and participating in community activities and monthly programs and by publishing and distributing printed materials."

FOCUS: Middle East. Human rights • women • international awareness • national liberation struggles • social justice • food, hunger, agribusiness.

ACTIVITIES: Popular education • political action • research and writing • solidarity work • networking • constituency education • library services • press service • documentation and dissemination of information • publishing • distribution of print matter • workshops and seminars • overseas project support.

RESOURCES: Speakers • audiovisuals • books and literature • consultant services.

PERIODICAL: *Najda Newsletter.* 6 issues/year.

Office of Women in International Development, University of Illinois at Urbana-Champaign, 801 S. Wright St., 324 Coble Hall, Champaign, IL 61820. Tel: (217) 333-1977.

"The Office of Women in International Development at UIUC is an academic unit concerned with increasing the awareness of and facilitating research in issues relating to women in the Third World, particularly with reference to the development process. The office organizes a seminar series and distributes a monthly newsletter during the academic year and develops and publishes curriculum guides on women and international development."

FOCUS: Third World general. Women • labor • food, hunger, agribusiness • development • technological change • education.

ACTIVITIES: Intern programs • library services • documentation and dissemination of information • workshops and seminars • curriculum development • research.

RESOURCES: Curriculum guides • speakers • consultant services.

PERIODICAL: *WID Information.* 9 issues/year. Newsletter.

Pacific and Asian Women's Forum, 4 Bhagwandas Rd., New Delhi 110 001, India.

"Pacific and Asian Women's Forum (PAWF) is an informal network of women activists, researchers, and other women concerned with and working on women's issues. PAWF was set up in 1977 with the objective of building a network of women's organisations and activities in the Asian and Pacific region to enable them to keep in touch with each other, cooperate in developing future programmes, and support each other in searching for solutions to common problems."

FOCUS: Asia and Pacific. Women • social justice.

ACTIVITIES: Documentation and dissemination of information • research and writing • networking • legislative action • policy-oriented research and writing • publisher.

RESOURCES: Books and literature • research services • consultant services.

PERIODICAL: *Pacific and Asian Women's Network Newsletter.*

Peoples Translation Service, 4228 Telegraph Ave., Oakland, CA 94609. Tel: (415) 654-6725.

"Peoples Translation Service publishes *Connexions* magazine and is beginning to organize an international women's resource center. *Connexions* brings information about women, often in their own words, into the United States in an attempt to unite the global women's movement."

FOCUS: Global • international. Women • labor • international awareness • social justice.

ACTIVITIES: Research and writing • media relations • library services • documentation and dissemination of information • publishing • distribution of print matter.

RESOURCES: Research services • books and literature • library.

PERIODICAL: *Connexions: An International Women's Quarterly.*

Third World Movement Against the Exploitation of Women (TW-MAE-W), P.O. Box 1434, Manila 2800, Philippines. Tel: 70 68 27.
"TW-MAE-W was constituted as an action-oriented, networking women's movement in January 1981. Emerging from early successes in its opposition to organized sex tours in Southeast Asia, the Third World Movement against the Exploitation of Women determined that the transnationalized approach to women's issues was an effective means for women to liberate themselves from the clutches of modern slavery and exploitation."

FOCUS: Third World general. Women • labor • transnational corporations • social justice • native peoples • food, hunger, agribusiness • prostitution • refugees • health.

ACTIVITIES: Political action • solidarity work • networking • publishing • workshops and seminars.

RESOURCES: Books and literature • research services • databank • research and occasional papers.

Woman to Woman, 5825 Telegraph Ave., P.O. Box A, Oakland, CA 94609. Tel: (415) 652-4400, ext. 419. Also at 444 Lincoln Blvd., P.O. Box 241, Venice, CA 90291; and 2520 N. Lincoln Ave., Box 196, Chicago, IL 60614. Tel: (312) 769-8079.
"This campaign was launched in October 1984 in order to support AMES (Women's Association of El Salvador) and AMNLAE (Luisa Amanda Espinosa Women's Association, Nicaragua). Our two main goals are to inform other women about the situation of women in Central America and to raise funds for AMES and AMNLAE. Funds raised go to support the rebuilding of childcare centers destroyed by the contras in Nicaragua, to build childcare centers in the liberated zones in El Salvador, and to care for refugee children at the Luz Dilian Arevalo Center in Managua, Nicaragua."

FOCUS: Nicaragua • El Salvador. Women • labor • social justice • food, hunger, agribusiness • health care • childcare.

ACTIVITIES: Political and material support • popular education • solidarity work • networking • publishing • distribution of audiovisuals.

RESOURCES: Audiovisuals • speakers.

PERIODICAL: Woman to Woman.

Women and Development Network of Australia, 262 Pitt St., 3rd fl., Sydney, NSW 2000, Australia. Regional offices in Adelaide, Brisbane, Canberra, Darwin, Hobart, Melbourne, and Perth.
"WADNA was begun in 1981 by Australian women working in the field of overseas aid and development. WADNA acts together with women of other countries to promote public awareness of issues concerning women internationally. We also work with Australian aid and development agencies to bring about better policies and programs which benefit women, are controlled by women, and take account of women's needs and rights."

FOCUS: Third World general • Asia and Pacific. Women • development • foreign aid • human rights • social justice.
ACTIVITIES: Popular education • political action • research and writing • solidarity work • networking • constituency education • policy-oriented research and writing • workshops and seminars.
RESOURCES: Speakers • research services • consultant services.
PERIODICAL: *Women and Development Newsletter.* 4 issues/year.

Women and Development Unit (WAND), University of the West Indies, Extra-Mural Department, Pinelands, St. Michael, Barbados.

"WAND was established as the result of a seminar on the Integration of Women in National Development in the Caribbean, held in Jamaica in June 1977 and attended by women representing the governments of the English-speaking countries of the Caribbean. The purpose of WAND is to monitor the Plan of Action developed at the seminar and to: provide training of trainers and resource persons; promote technical assistance programs; publish and distribute materials; and develop research programs and programs for legislative change."

FOCUS: Caribbean. Women • labor • social justice • food, hunger, agribusiness • health • development • education • communications.
ACTIVITIES: Community development • popular education • research and writing • media relations • networking • documentation and dissemination of information • publishing • workshops and seminars • technical assistance • project support.
RESOURCES: Curriculum guides • research services • consultant services • library.
PERIODICAL: *Woman Speak!*

Women for Guatemala, P.O. Box 53421, 1618 V St., NW, Washington, DC 20009. Tel: (202) 234–6037.

"Women for Guatemala works to promote an understanding of the condition of women in Guatemala today and to sponsor actions, such as writing and advertising campaigns, that can assist these women."

FOCUS: Latin America and Caribbean. Women • labor • political economy • national liberation struggles • social justice • native peoples • food, hunger, agribusiness • Guatemalan Indian women.
ACTIVITIES: Popular education • solidarity work • media relations • film and slideshow maker • constituency education • documentation and dissemination of information • publishing • distribution of print matter.
RESOURCES: Audiovisuals • study-action guides • research services • books and literature • news reports.
PERIODICAL: *Ch'Abuj Ri Ixoc: The Voice of the Women.*

Women in International Development, Michigan State University, 202 Center for International Programs, East Lansing, MI 48824–1035. Tel: (517) 353–5040.

"MSU/WID is a coordinating unit that focuses on the roles of women in economic, social, and political contexts. Through exchange relationships with women's organizations both in the United States and abroad,

MSU/WID has compiled an extensive library of materials. MSU/WID publishes two series, *Women in International Development* and the *WID Forum*, that are widely disseminated to individuals, agencies, universities, and other national and international public institutions. The *WID Bulletin*, a newsletter published three times a year, carries information about events, conferences, resources, practitioners, and policy makers in the field."

FOCUS: Third World general. Women • labor • political economy • social justice • food, hunger, agribusiness.

ACTIVITIES: Research and writing • intern programs • networking • constituency education • policy-oriented research and writing • library services • documentation and dissemination of information • publishing • distribution of print matter • distribution of audiovisuals.

RESOURCES: Speakers • books and literature • consultant services • library • working papers • short reports.

PERIODICAL: *WID Bulletin.*

Women Strike for Peace, National Office, 145 S. 13 St., Philadelphia, PA 19107. Tel: (215) 923-0861. Regional offices in New York, Los Angeles, San Francisco, Seattle, Washington, D.C., Berkeley, and Chicago.

"Founded in 1961 Women Strike for Peace works to achieve international disarmament under effective controls; to ban nuclear testing, to end the arms race and abolish all weapons of destruction, with safeguards enforced by a strengthened United Nations; and to join with women throughout the world to challenge the right of any nation or groups of nations to hold the power of life or death over the world."

FOCUS: Global. Women • militarism, peace, disarmament • nuclear arms and energy.

ACTIVITIES: Media • popular education • research and writing • legislative action • Congressional testimony • leafletting • public meetings.

RESOURCES: Speakers.

Women's International League for Peace and Freedom, 1213 Race St., Philadelphia, PA 19107. Tel: (215) 563-7110.

"Through its national network WILPF works to eliminate the economic and social causes of oppression through social change. In this way the League hopes to end the arms race, militarism, U.S. intervention abroad, government repression, sexism, and racism."

FOCUS: International. Women • national liberation struggles • transnational corporations • United Nations • civil liberties • nonviolence.

ACTIVITIES: Popular education • political action • networking • legislative action • study groups • public meetings.

RESOURCES: Speakers • books and literature • consultant services.

PERIODICAL: *Peace and Freedom.* 12 issues/year. Membership newsletter.

Women's International Network, 187 Grant St., Lexington, MA 02173. Tel: (617) 862-9431.

"Women's International Network is a worldwide, open communication system run by, for, and about women of all backgrounds, beliefs, nationalities, and age groups. WIN's quarterly magazine serves the general public, institutions, and organizations by transmitting internationally information about women and women's groups. WIN has produced the highly acclaimed and widely distributed *Universal Childbirth Picture Book* — a picture story of reproduction from a woman's view, as well as numerous publications on the genital/sexual mutilation of females."

FOCUS: Global. Women • international awareness • social justice • food, hunger, agribusiness • development (in the broadest sense) of women.

ACTIVITIES: Popular education • media relations • constituency education • Congressional testimony • documentation and dissemination of information • publishing • health education.

RESOURCES: Speakers • audiovisuals • research services • books and literature • consultant services.

PERIODICAL: *WIN News.*

Women's International Resource Exchange, 2700 Broadway, Rm. 7, New York, NY 10025. Tel: (212) 666-4622.

"WIRE publishes and distributes, nationally and internationally, writings by Third World women."

FOCUS: Third World general. Women • labor • political economy • international awareness • national liberation struggles • transnational corporations • social justice • native peoples • food, hunger, agribusiness.

ACTIVITIES: Popular education • intern programs • media relations • networking • film and slideshow production • constituency education • documentation and dissemination of information • publishing • distribution of print matter • workshops and seminars • overseas project support.

RESOURCES: Speakers • audiovisuals • books and literature.

Women's International Self-Education Resource Links, 173 Archway Rd., London, N16 5AB England.

"Begun in 1983 this international women's resource center seeks to promote awareness of women's importance in economic, political, and social development by way of articles, evening courses, conferences, the production of educational materials, and by providing access to specialized library resources. A bimonthly newsletter, *Wiser Links*, promotes dialogue and encourages direct links between women and organizations with similiar concerns in Western and Third World countries."

FOCUS: International. Women • political economy • development.

ACTIVITIES: Networking • popular education • solidarity work • library services • workshops and seminars • overseas project support • curriculum development.

RESOURCES: Library • bookstore • curriculum guides.
PERIODICAL: *Wiser Links.*

SUPPLEMENTARY LIST OF ORGANIZATIONS

AFRICA

African National Congress, Women's Section, P.O. Box 31791, Lusaka, Zambia.
African Training and Research Centre for Women, P.O. Box 3001, Addis Ababa, Ethiopia.
African Women's Features Service, P.O. Box 74536, Nairobi, Kenya.
Association for Women Solidarity, 25 Murad St., Giza, Egypt. Tel: 723976.
Association of African Women for Research and Development (AAWORD), B.P. 11007, CD Annexe, Dakar, Senegal.
Council for the Development of Economic and Social Research in Africa (CODESRIA), B.P. 3304, Dakar, Senegal.
Federation of African Media Women, c/o Zimbabwe Inter-Africa News Agency, P.O. Box 8166, Causeway, Harare, Zimbabwe.
Maendeleo Ya Wanawake Organisation, P.O. Box 44412, Nairobi, Kenya.
Mazingira Institute, P.O. Box 14550, Nairobi, Kenya.
South African Council of Churches, Home and Family Life, Women's Desk, P.O. Box 4921, Johannesburg 2000, South Africa.
Zimbabwe Publishing House, P.O. Box BW 350, Borrowdale, Harare, Zimbabwe.
Zimbabwe Women's Bureau, 152b Victoria St., Salisbury, Zimbabwe.

ASIA AND PACIFIC

Asian and Pacific Centre for Women and Development, Asian and Pacific Development Centre, Pesiaran Duta, P.O. Box 2224, Kuala Lumpur, Malaysia.
Asian-Pacific Women's Network, c/o ACFOD, P.O. Box 2930, Bangkok 10500, Thailand.

Asian Women's Association, c/o Nishihara Church, 76 Aza Goya, Nishihara-cho, Okinawa 903–01, Japan.

Asian Women's Institute, c/o Lucknow Publishing House, 37 Cantonment Rd., Lucknow, India.

Asian Women's Research and Action Network, c/o Philipina, P.O. Box 208, Davao City 9501, Philippines. Tel: 77–53–41. Also at 12 Pasaje dela Paz, Project 4, Quezon City, Philippines. Tel: 77–53–41.

Association of Christian Institutes for Social Concern in Asia, Kansai Seminar House, 23 Takenouchi-cho, Ichijoji, Sakyo-ku, Kyoto 606, Japan.

Centre for Women's Development Studies, B–43, Panchsheel Enclave, New Delhi 110017, India.

Centre for Women's Research, Attn: Swarna Jayaweer & Hema Goonatilake, 120/10 Wijerama Mawatha, Colombo 7, Sri Lanka.

Depth News Women's Features Services, P.O. Box 1843, Manila, Philippines.

GABRIELA (General Assembly Binding Women for Reforms, Integrity, Equality, Leadership, and Action), Rm. 221, PCI Bldg., Greenhills Commercial Center, San Juan, Metro Manila, Philippines.

Indian Council of Social Science Research, Women's Studies Programme, IIPA Hostel, Indraprastha Estate, Ring Rd., New Delhi 110002, India.

Indian Social Institute, Programme for Women's Development, Lodi Rd., New Delhi 110003, India.

Institute for Social Research and Education, Carol Mansion, 35 Sitladevi Temple Rd., Mahim, Bombay 400016, India.

Kanita Project, Universiti Sains Malaysia, School of Social Sciences, Penang, Malaysia.

Pakistan Women's Institute, 93 Jail Rd., Lahore, Pakistan.

Voice of Women, 16/1, Don Carolis Rd., Colombo, 5 Sri Lanka.

Women for Women, Road no. 4, House no. 67, Dhanmondi R.A., Dacca, Bangladesh.

Women's Action for Development, D–139 Anand Niketan, New Delhi 110021, India.

Women's Centre, 307 Yasmeen Apartment, Yeshwant Nagar, Vakola, Santacruz (W), Bombay 400055, India.

Women's Information Center, 2/3 Soi Wan Lang, Arunamarin Rd., Bangkok 10700, Thailand.

Women's Link, Women's Concern Desk, Christian Conference of Asia, 480, Lorong 2, Toa Payoh, Singapore 1231, Singapore.

EUROPE

Alliance Internationale des Femmes (IAF), P.O. Box 355, Valetta, Malta.

Associazione Italiana Donne per lo Sviluppo, Piazza Capranica 95, interno 4, 00186 Rome, Italy.

Centre for Development Research, 9 Ny Kongensgade, 1472 Copenhagen K, Denmark.

Centro de Estudios 'Elsa Bergamaschi,' Via della Colonna Antonina 41, Rome, Italy.

Collectif des Femmes Maghrebines, c/o Maison des Femmes, 8 Cité Prost, 75011 Paris, France.

Concerned Asian Women, Pernambucodreef 27, 3563 CS Utrecht, Netherlands. Tel: 030-620221.

Fédération Démocratique Internationale des Femmes, 13 Unter den Linden, D-1080 Berlin, East Germany.

Institute of Development Studies, Program on Women and Development, University of Sussex, Brighton BN1 9RE, England.

Institute of Social Studies, Women's Studies Programme, Badhuisweg 251, 2597 JR The Hague, Netherlands.

Kvinfo, Leaderstraede 15, 2 Sal., DK-1201 Copenhagen K, Denmark.

Officina Informativa de la Mujer, c/o Interpress Service, Via Panisperna 207, Rome, Italy.

Progressive Women's Organization, Faelledvej 16C, 4. tv., DK-2200 Copenhagen, Denmark.

UNESCO Population Division, 7, place de Fontenoy, 75700 Paris, France.

United Nations Industrial Development Organization, Program for Women, Vienna International Centre, P.O. Box 300, A-1400 Vienna, Austria.

Women and Work Hazards Group, British Society for Social Responsibility in Science, 9 Poland St., London W1, England.

Women's Research and Resource Centre, 190 Upper St., London N1, England.

Women's Research Centre in Social Science, H.C. Andersens Blvd. 38, Mezz., DK-1553, Copenhagen V, Denmark.

Workgroup on Prostitution Tourism and Traffic in Women, c/o MIAC, Voor Clarenburg 10, Utrecht, Netherlands.

World Council of Churches, Women's Desk, 1211 Geneva 20, Switzerland.

LATIN AMERICA AND CARIBBEAN

Associação de Mulheres Mato Grosso, Rua Baltazar Navarro 231, Bandeirante, 78,000 Cuiabá-Mato Grosso, Brazil.

Caribbean Women's Feature Syndicate, P.O. Box 159, Bridgetown, Barbados.

Centro de Estudios de la Mujer, Olleros 2554 - P.B., 1426 Buenos Aires, Argentina.

Centro de Información y Recursos para la Mujer, Calle 36, No. 17–44, Bogotá, Colombia. Tel: 287–2319.

Centro de Investigación para la Acción Femenina (CIPAF), Apartado Postal 1744, Santo Domingo DN, Dominican Republic.

Centro de la Mujer Peruana 'Flora Tristán,' Jirón Quilca 431, 100 Lima, Peru.

Centro Dominicano de Estudios de la Educación, Juan Sánchez Ramírez No. 41, Santo Domingo, Dominican Republic.

Cine Mujer, Apartado Aereo 2758, Bogotá, Colombia.

Circulos Femeninos Populares, Apartado 4240, 1010–A Caracas, Venezuela.

Comunicación, Intercambio y Desarrollo Humano en América Latina (CIDHAL), Apartado Postal 579, Cuernavaca, Morelos, Mexico.

Fundação Carlos Chagas Women's Program, Avenida Prof. Francisco Morato 1565, 05513 São Paulo SP, Brazil.

IXQUIC, Apartado Postal 27–008, Mexico 06760, DF, Mexico.

Lugar de Mujer, Corrientes 2817, 5B, 1193 Buenos Aires, Argentina.

Mujer-Tec, Apartado Postal 284–9, Los Ríos, Santo Domingo, Dominican Republic.

MIDDLE EAST

General Arab Women Federation, Hay Al-Maghreb, Mahaela 304, Zuqaq 5/33, Baghdad, Iraq.

Women against the Occupation, P.O. Box 2760, Tel Aviv, Israel.

NORTH AMERICA

AAUW Educational Foundation, 2401 Virginia Ave., NW, Washington, DC 20037.

Center for Women's Studies and Services, 908 E St., San Diego, CA 92101.

Coalition of Canadian Women's Groups, International Peace Conference, Rm. 9–10, Seton Anne, 166 Bedford Hwy., Halifax, NS B3M 2J6, Canada.

Committee on Women in Asian Studies (CWAS), 409 Maxwell Hall, Syracuse University, Syracuse, NY 13210. Tel: (315) 423–3114.

National Institute for Women of Color, 1712 N St., NW, Washington, DC 20036.

Presbyterian Church (USA), Third World Women's Coordinating Committee, 475 Riverside Dr., Rm. 1164, New York, NY 10115. Tel: (212) 870–2885.

Secretariat for Women in Development, New TransCentury Foundation, 1789 Columbia Rd., NW, Washington, DC 20009.

Third World Women's Archives, P.O. Box 159, Bush Terminal Sta., Brooklyn, NY 11232. Tel: (212) 308–5389.

United Methodist Church, Women's Division, 475 Riverside Dr., New York, NY 10115.

Women and Development Working Group, Canadian Council for International Cooperation, 450 Rideau St., Ottawa, Ontario K1N 5Z4, Canada.

Women in the World, Curriculum Resource Project, 1030 Spruce St., Berkeley, CA 94707. Tel: (415) 524–0304.

Women in World Area Studies, c/o Susan Gross or Marjorie Bingham, 6425 W. 33 St., St. Louis Park, MN 55426. Tel: (612) 925–3632.

Women's Information Network, 1710 Connecticut Ave., NW, Washington, DC 20036.

Women's Institute for Freedom of the Press, 3306 Ross Pl., NW, Washington, DC 20008. Tel: (202) 966–7783.

Women's Research and Resource Centre, 252 Bloor St. W., Toronto, Ontario M5S 1V6, Canada. Tel: (416) 597–8865.

INFORMATION SOURCES

The organizations included in this directory are for the most part focused directly on women in the Third World. Organizations such as Amnesty International, Clergy and Laity Concerned, and the Data Center are not included because their interests and resources are broader than this one issue. These organizations do, however, include the special concerns of women in their educational programs and resources and they should, therefore, be contacted. For information on such groups, see the bibliographies, guides, and reference books described in the books chapter below, as well as these resources:

From **Third World Resources**, 464 19 St., Oakland, CA 94612:

Asia and Pacific: A Directory of Resources. Compiled and edited by Thomas P. Fenton and Mary J. Heffron. Maryknoll, N.Y., and London: Orbis Books and Zed Books, 1986. 160pp. $9.95, plus $1.50 shipping and handling. Illustrations and indexes.

Latin America and Caribbean: A Directory of Resources. Compiled and edited by Thomas P. Fenton and Mary J. Heffron. Maryknoll, N.Y., and London: Orbis Books and Zed Books, 1986. 160pp. $9.95, plus $1.50 shipping and handling. Illustrations and indexes.

Resource directories on Africa and on the Middle East are forthcoming from Orbis and Zed in 1987.

Third World Resource Directory: A Guide to Organizations and Publications. Edited by Thomas P. Fenton and Mary J. Heffron. Maryknoll, N.Y.: Orbis Books, 1984. 304pp. $17.95, plus $1.50 shipping and handling. Illustrations, indexes.

The organizations section (pp. 222–24) of the chapter on women should be consulted, along with the listings of organizations in the other nine chapters.

Third World Resources: A Quarterly Review of Resources from and about the Third World. 4 issues/year. Newsletter. 28cm. 16pp. $25/year (organizational subscription), $25/two years (individual subscription). Inquire for overseas rates. Subscriptions are available on a calendar-year basis only.

From **Human Rights Internet,** c/o Harvard Law School, Pound Hall, Rm. 401, Cambridge, MA 02138:

Human Rights Directory: Latin America, Africa, Asia. 1981. 244pp. $22.50. Indexes. *Update.* 1985. 50pp. $5.

North American Human Rights Directory. 1984. 264pp. $30. Indexes.

Western Europe Human Rights Directory. 1982. 335pp. $30. Indexes.

The resources given below are concerned particularly with women in the Third World:

From **International Women's Tribune Centre,** 777 United Nations Plaza, New York, NY 10017:

A Guide to Women's Centres in Latin America. 1986. 224pp. $8. In Spanish.

Mid-Decade Directory. Five regional booklets. 1980. $5 per set.

These five directories contain the names and addresses of participants at the Non-Governmental Organization (NGO) Mid-Decade Forum and World Conference of the UN Decade for Women, Copenhagen, Denmark, July 14–28, 1980.

Women Organizing. September 1984. 114pp.

A collection of IWTC newsletters on women's organizing and networking strategies.

In addition, see the directories and guides listed in the books chapter below and periodicals such as *Connexions, Feminist Collections, Isis International Women's Bulletin,* and *WIN News* that regularly list and describe international women's organizations.

2

Books

This chapter is divided into three parts: annotated entries, supplementary list of books, and sources of additional information on books related to women in the Third World. Annotated entries are divided into five sections: general; bibliographies; catalogs, directories, guides; study guides and curriculum materials; and reference books.

Information in the **annotated entries** is given in the following order: author(s) or editor(s); title; place of publication; publisher; date of publication; number of pages; price; keyword description of format; description of content.

Books in the **supplementary list** (pp. 50–53) are grouped under these headings: Third World; Africa; Asia and Pacific; Latin America and Caribbean; and Middle East. Information in the entries in this section is given in the following order: author(s) or editor(s); title; place of publication; publisher; date of publication; number of pages; price.

The **information sources** section (pp. 53–54) provides the names of directories and guides that contain the titles of other books related to women in the Third World.

All titles are integrated into the titles index at the back of the directory. The addresses for most of the publishers and distributors appear in the organizations index. (We have omitted addresses when we judged that a particular book could be easily acquired through a bookstore or library.) We have given the North American distributors for books published outside the United States. Readers in other countries should check with publishers for local distributors.

All books are paperback unless we indicate that they are clothbound.

ANNOTATED ENTRIES

General

Andreas, Carol. *When Women Rebel: The Rise of Popular Feminism in Peru*. Westport, Conn.: Lawrence Hill, 1985. 234pp. $12.95. Notes and references, photographs, glossary.

Longtime educator and activist Carol Andreas admits from the start that hers is not a "balanced" view of Peruvian history or of women's movements in Peru. "Rather," she says, "I have tried to emphasize the often hidden aspects of history that are crucial to the interpretation of social change. Many people who have some acquaintance with Peruvian political developments, even those who are themselves Peruvians, who are themselves women, or who consider themselves scholars or revolutionaries, lack an understanding of the sources of the collective power of women in Peru. Most know little or nothing about the forms of struggle and the ways of thinking of those women who are politically active in the barriadas of the cities and in the indigenous communities of the countryside and the jungle, or of those women who work in the streets or in private homes or industries, thereby serving the needs of 'development' without reaping any of its benefits."

"What I have done," Andreas states, "is to document information that has been systematically kept from the public, especially from the women who are themselves most likely to be affected. This information does not consist of scattered facts or isolated events. On the contrary, I have purposely sought to include facts and events that I believe are highly determinative in the history of women and in the history of Peru. In making them more visible, I seek to make them more determinative."

While refraining from extravagant claims about the degree of her intimacy with the women of Peru, Andreas does reveal enough about her years of experience in Peru to convince us that she speaks with a great deal of personal knowledge and concern about women in Peru's rural area and urban shantytowns and about subjects such as native revival, popular struggle, and feminism in Peru. Her personal renditions of history and her stories of present-day struggles for national and women's liberation are effectively augmented by forty-four photographs.

Atiya, Nayra. *Khul-Khaal: Five Egyptian Women Tell Their Stories.* **Syracuse, N.Y.: Syracuse University Press, 1982. 178pp. $11.95. Photographs.**

U.S.-educated writer, poet, and painter Nayra Atiya has gathered oral histories from five Egyptian women who share much in common: they all reside in an urban environment; they are all in one way or another attempting to survive "in the monied economy of city life"; all but one comes from the lower social class; and all but one never received more than a primary school education.

"The women have in common," Atiya adds, "their extraordinary natural perception about the world in which we live. The stories provide us with a rich mine of materials on which to reflect. These are not specially talented storytellers—rather they have absorbed the narrative skills that are particularly developed among the folk of Egypt. When we listen to the women talking about their lives, we get a sense that they have brooded a great deal over their destinies. There is a philosophical breadth and eloquence to the narratives—a richness of expression—that one might not expect in people of such substandard physical environments. These women are philosophers."

Atiya characterizes the stories she collected in these words: "Better than analytical models, these stories give the meaning of kinship structures, decision-making vectors, cultural symbols, systems of obligations and rights, and of economic and social adaptation to particular environments. They show concepts, world view, domestic cycle regularities, and values and norms without the technical terms that reduce these processes to cold and formal dimensions."

The stories in *Khul-Khaal* present an unsettling challenge to Westerners, who, Atiya believes, "have come too quickly to expect that ours are the international expectations of feminism—that other women will come to want the same rights and goals we seek—or, that once a society is frankly dominated in certain spheres by men, women will be a suppressed and passive group." "Nothing could be further from the truth," Atiya concludes, "as the pages of this book indicate. What is important to understand is how such seeming contradictions by western standards can be reconciled into a way of life that is both consistent and fulfilling to a large portion of Egyptians, male and female."

The *khul-khaal* of the book's title are heavy silver or gold anklets worn by married women. Atiya explains that though they resemble shackles, they can also be used to advantage—as items that can be sold in times of extreme need or can be used to call attention seductively to the wearer.

Barry, Kathleen, Charlotte Bunch, and Shirley Castley, eds. *International Feminism: Networking against Female Sexual Slavery.* **New York: International Women's Tribune Centre, 1984. 142pp. $6. List of participants, photographs, notes, bibliography, list of resources, appendixes.**

This report of a workshop on female sexual slavery held in Rotterdam (April 6–15, 1983), a follow-up to a study group at the Copenhagen 1980 Mid-Decade Conference on Women, presents "the working and thinking" of "committed individuals and groups around the world" on "female sexual slavery and violence against women." It also considers ways of further publicizing these issues and of bringing them "into political focus."

The editors see prostitution not as "an isolated phenomenon," but as "another form of that sexual violence to which many women are subjected daily as battered wives, political prisoners, refugees, etc." In their introduction they admit that there will be "no simple end to the practices discussed here because they involve complex patterns of sexual, economic, cultural, and political exploitation of women over many centuries." They believe, however, that "there will never be solutions unless we expose and oppose these practices at every level and in every way possible."

The editors' exposition of the problem consists in well-documented descriptions and analyses of female sexual slavery from regions throughout the world. There is no area in the world, the editors state, "where this problem does not exist, and there is no area in the world where women are not being degraded in the process of trafficking and forced prostitution."

The strength and determination of those who oppose female sexual slavery is evident throughout the papers in this book that discuss efforts to "bring together and utilize existing groups and resources . . . to create more effective cooperation among groups that are already at work in areas related to female sexual slavery."

Bendt, Ingela, and James Downing. *We Shall Return: Women of Palestine.* **Trans. Ann Henning. London: Zed Books, 1982. 144pp. $8.50. Map, tables, photographs, chronology. Available in the United States from Biblio Distribution Center (Totowa, N.J.).**

This on-site investigation of the situation of Palestinian women in Lebanon by two freelance journalists from Sweden met with two responses. The first, from a headmaster in the village of Souk al Gharb: "For you, in the West, women's circumstances are a luxury to investigate; here we're fighting for our lives!" The second, from a young woman in the Palestinian Women's Association: "It's about time. . . . All the time we are the ones who sacrifice and suffer the most. . . . The woman carries two-thirds of the social responsibility; the man carries the rest."

Bendt and Downing offer a moving portrait of Palestinian women — their day-to-day struggles in Lebanon's refugee camps and their efforts to create a homeland for the Palestinian people. As if in response to one Palestinian woman's dismay that foreigners want "to give *their* picture of events, not ours," *We Shall Return* lets the women speak for themselves.

Um Leila, one of the last women the authors interviewed before leaving Lebanon, captured the steadfast dedication of the Palestinian women: "One final thing, one thing you must mention in your book. Write that in spite of all the obstacles, in spite of war and death, in spite of the opposition from the men, the Palestinian women will participate in the liberation struggle. . . . Without the women the Revolution would be without a future."

Bronstein, Audrey. *Triple Struggle: Latin American Peasant Women.* **Boston: South End, 1983. 272pp. $7.50. Recommended readings list, photographs, maps, statistical tables, glossary.**

Peasant women in Latin America suffer in three ways, writes community developer Bronstein: "as citizens of underdeveloped countries; as peasants, living in the most impoverished and disadvantaged areas of those countries; and as women, in male-dominated societies."

In an effort to document this threefold suffering and to give voice to the concerns of "the most silent of all Latin Americans — peasant indigenous women," Bronstein traveled widely in four countries where Indians still make up the majority of the population (Guatemala, Ecuador, Peru, and Bolivia), as well as in El Salvador. "I hoped to speak with women, who, within a peasant, macho society, rarely speak, or give their opinions publicly on anything, much less on their own living conditions and the changes introduced by both foreign and indigenous development agencies."

Bronstein also hoped "to learn about the role of women in the struggle for social and economic change in the Third World" and "to compare the concerns of Third World women with our own in industrialised nations."

The author's yearlong stay in Latin America led her to conclude that "although the women interviewed were separated geographically by thousands of miles, and culturally by different languages and traditions, their concerns and experiences were remarkably similar. In spite of regional differences existing within countries, down to differences between families in one village and sisters in one family, the women repeatedly described one factor common to them all: their oppression—at work, in the community and in the family. They shared, too, a belief in their own inferiority and saw themselves as having no real choice for change in their lives."

"The oppression of Latin American peasant women," Bronstein continues, "is not simply the result of a set of complex economic and social circumstances that make, and keep, them poor. It also functions through the roles conferred on them and attitudes directed towards them by virtue of their sex. They are oppressed because they are women."

Each chapter of *The Triple Struggle* is devoted to one country and each begins with a brief introduction to the political, economic, and social characteristics of the nation, including a map and statistical tables. The remainder of the chapter is given to reports of women's struggles—most often in the words of the women themselves.

Bunster, Ximena, and Elsa M. Chaney. *Sellers and Servants: Working Women in Lima, Peru.* **Photography by Ellan Young. New York and London: Praeger, 1985. 258pp. $35.95. Cloth. Glossary, tables, photographs, bibliography, index.**

Nearly one-third of all employed women in Latin America are sellers or servants. In Lima, Peru—the site of this study—nearly one-half of the employed women work in those occupations. The occupations are critical subjects of study not only because of their numerical importance but also because those jobs occupy the lower tiers of the traditional labor market both in terms of wages and conditions of work. Yet, until this study little was known about the women who labored as sellers and servants in Latin America.

"Why are so many Third World women and men still earning their livelihood in such seemingly haphazard fashion, after more than two decades of intensive development activity?" the authors ask. And what about the evidence that shows that even when Third World women do get jobs in the modern sector, they are condemned to work in crowded, unsanitary, and noisy conditions at repetitive jobs in the branches of transnational corporations?

Using a pioneer "talking pictures" interviewing technique, the authors of this study (a Chilean anthropologist and an international development specialist) have amassed a fascinating body of information on poor working women in Lima and—it is to be hoped—have made a considerable contribution to the emancipation of the subjects of their study and of women in other Third World cities as well.

Burgos-Debray, Elisabeth, ed. *I . . . Rigoberta Menchú: An Indian Woman in Guatemala*. London: Verso/NLB, 1984. 200pp. $8.95.

"My story is the story of all poor Guatemalans. My personal experience is the reality of a whole people . . . the testimony of my people." So begins the moving story of Rigoberta Menchú, a Quiché Indian woman of Guatemala.

Invited to Europe by solidarity groups, she is put in touch with Elisabeth Burgos-Debray for the purpose of making her life story into a book. The work began with the taping of Rigoberta Menchú's own words in intensive daily conversations with Burgos-Debray. Then followed the precise and complete transcription of these tapes into 500 typed pages. Burgos-Debray has sensitively and respectfully arranged the whole thematically and chronologically, using a monologue form and thus allowing the real author to truly and simply speak for herself and her people. "The voice of Rigoberta Menchú allows the defeated to speak," writes the editor in her introduction.

Rigoberta Menchú is a "privileged witness," a survivor first of the poverty of her people and then of the outright genocide that destroyed her family and her community. Her father is now a national hero of the Indians of Guatemala. He was the leader of a group who occupied the Spanish embassy in Guatemala City in January 1981. The group was massacred. The hero's daughter is now a leader of her people, an organizer and spokesperson. She has chosen "words as her weapon."

The major themes of Rigoberta Menchú's story are father, mother, childhood, death, education, work, relations with *ladinos*, and linguistic problems. Special emphasis is given to cultural customs and practices.

This is, as Burgos-Debray says, an "overwhelming" story, and it is so because it is true.

***Central American Women Speak for Themselves*. Toronto: Latin American Working Group, October 1983. 104pp. $7, plus 20 percent for handling. Bulk rates available. Maps, illustrations, tables, photographs, list of resources.**

This dossier of translations from newspapers, pamphlets, documents, and reports focuses on "the participation of women in the popular movements and revolutionary organizations which are so important at this moment in Central American history." Three countries are included: Nicaragua, El Salvador, and Guatemala.

"In some cases," the editors write, "women participate in women's organizations, such as AMNLAE [the Nicaraguan women's organization]. In other cases, women are working actively within their unions, *barrio* committees, markets, churches. Some women participate in the committees of the mothers of political prisoners and the disappeared. Women's involvement ranges from protesting the consumerization of Christmas, to carrying messages to guerrilla organizations, to struggling for maternity benefits, to fighting in military fronts."

This dossier, published by the highly regarded Latin American Working Group, contains the stories of some of these women. These are special stories, the editors explain: "As women, and in many cases, as indigenous women, they have tremendous obstacles to overcome in order to actively participate in political or economic life. Illiteracy and poverty, as well as a great deal of backward thinking about women's roles, have relegated many women to positions little better than beasts of burden." The stories describe these obstacles and tell how women — even those from different backgrounds — are working together to overcome them.

Chapkis, Wendy, and Cynthia Enloe, eds. *Of Common Cloth: Women in the Global Textile Industry.* **Washington, D.C.: Institute for Policy Studies, 1983. 141pp. $5.95.**

This book is the fruit of a three-day meeting held at the Transnational Institute in Amsterdam that brought together women from several First and Third World countries — researchers, trade unionists, activists, and others — "to exchange experiences and information on the fast-changing global textile industry." Basic to the meeting was the knowledge that women supply much of the labor power, in unskilled, low-paid, deadend jobs in one of the world's "oldest and most fundamental industries," the textile industry, and the belief that women needed to get a "clearer understanding of how their exploitation is rooted in the structures and mythologies of sexism."

In compiling this reader, explain the editors, "we had before us the images of women — separated by country and culture — each working her bit of fabric. This book is intended to take those separate experiences and begin to weave them into a piece of common cloth."

The book addresses such topics as the myths about women as workers (that they are docile, that they don't need to earn as much as men, that they don't mind monotony, that they have naturally nimble fingers); women's place in the international division of labor ("cheap labor" means women's labor); the patriarchal thread running through the history of the textile industry; conditions in India, Philippines, Mexico, and South Korea; women as workers in the home and in the factory; technology; safety; racism; organizing strikes and devising strategies; and union-busting.

Important issues are thus raised, but they are not developed. The book serves to whet one's appetite and is a good introduction to women's role in this important industry and in the worldwide labor system. The resource section supplies useful suggestions for further reading and action.

Christian Conference of Asia–Urban Rural Mission. *Struggling to Survive: Women Workers in Asia.* **Hongkong: CCA–URM, 1983. 162pp. $1. Photographs, illustrations, tables, maps.**

This short book contains stories of Asian women who are industrial workers in Hongkong, Thailand, Malaysia, Sri Lanka, and the Philippines. Case studies describe the low wages, long working hours, and inhumane treatment that are the lot of these women. Each section opens with a short essay that puts the stories into a national and historical context.

Cutrufelli, Maria Rosa. *Women of Africa: Roots of Oppression.* **London: Zed Books, 1983. 192pp. $9.25. Tables, notes, bibliography. Available in the United States from Biblio Distribution Center (Totowa, N.J.).**

In her lengthy introduction to the English edition of this book Italian author and sociologist Cutrufelli states her belief that "women throughout the world should now, more than ever, surmount any cultural, racial, and historical divide between them and learn to know one another better."

Women of Africa is Maria Rosa Cutrufelli's contribution to greater understanding of the women of Africa. She describes the colonial period, pointing out how colonial domination changed the complex and diverse web of family ties and relations between the sexes as expressed in marriage rites, dowries, polygamy, inheritance, and various other aspects of family and kinship systems.

The author then turns her critical eye to the changing situation of women in postcolonial Africa. She analyzes conditions of work both in rural and urban settings, job opportunities for women, domestic labor, and the recent growth of prostitution. Issues having to do with women's control over their own bodies – clitoridectomy, contraception, abortion, and motherhood – are also studied. Finally, Cutrufelli discusses African women's growing participation in social struggles and political movements on the continent.

Though she denounces the many ways that traditional and colonial societies have oppressed women the author is no less critical in her examination of the ways in which black nationalist leaders have manipulated the rights and demands of women to fit their purposes. She attacks, as well, the way that the new African states "have generally adopted the colonial policies of utilizing the female labour force in the subsistence sector of the economy, and male force in the modern sector." "Obviously," she concludes, "such policy of sexual division of labour has impoverished women, and not just literally. They have been penned inside a society which, rather than traditional, should now be labelled backward and subordinate, and tied down to behaviour and modes of being which impede their efforts for emancipation."

The author – a feminist and a Marxist – has researched the position of women in underdeveloped parts of the world, notably southern Italy and Africa – for many years. *Women of Africa* is hard-hitting, well-documented, and sophisticated in its political arguments.

el Dareer, Asma. *Woman, Why Do You Weep? Circumcision and Its Consequences.* **London: Zed Books, 1983. 130pp. $7.50. Map, tables, photographs, bibliography, appendixes. Available in the United States from Biblio Distribution Center (Totowa, N.J.).**

Asma el Dareer, a Sudanese medical doctor who has long been involved in health and development work in her country, presents in this book the results of a statistical survey she conducted in the northern provinces of the Sudan on the widespread practice of female circumcision. Deeply moved as much by her younger sister's circumcision as by her own at the age of eleven, Dr. el Dareer has devoted her life and professional skills to understanding, publicizing, and combating this terrible practice. Circumcision, she states, is "not simply an operation of a few minutes duration after which it is all over, but the subsequent complications [both physiological and psychological] exist until the end of a woman's lifetime."

The chapters of *Woman, Why Do You Weep?* correspond to the objectives of the survey that she outlines in her introduction: "(1) To determine the prevalence of the practice and types of female circumcision in the Sudan; (2) To identify the resulting health problems; and (3) To outline the social, religious, and traditional attitudes towards the custom and hence to discuss possible ways which could lead to its eradication."

"Attempts to prohibit the circumcision of women," the doctor writes at the opening of her final chapter, "only began in comparatively recent times." "Possibly," she says, "this is because the custom is very old and deeply rooted and also because, like many customs, it was accepted without question. No one dared to examine its malevolent effects or even — it seems — to be fully aware of them." She describes attempts that have been made to curb or abolish the practice and then sets forth her own recommendations for action, including education and legislation.

Davies, Carole Boyce, and Anne Adams Graves, eds. *Ngambika: Studies of Women In African Literature.* **Trenton, N.J.: Africa World Press, 1986. 298pp. $11.95. Notes, references, bibliography, annotated list of bibliographies, notes on contributors.**

The compilers of these eighteen critical analyses of literature about African women state that their aim is "to redress the relative inattention to women in African literary scholarship," and, thereby, to expand and augment "the interpretation of the whole body of African literary creativity." "This objective," they state, "involves both a re-reading of earlier writings, produced entirely by men, and a balanced reading of the more recent writings by women and by men."

Editor Graves then expands upon the above statements by stressing the concern of the critics who contributed to this volume that "the perspective and characterization of women, heretofore relegated to the critical shadows, be brought into focus in whatever form they may manifest themselves in the works." "The issue in this book," she writes, "is the opening up of the critical perspective, to look at woman in African literature standing on her own rather than in the shadow of the men with whom she shares the literary stage."

The literary works studied in this anthology come from several areas of the African continent — East, West, Central, South, and the Maghreb — and cover numerous language groups, religious belief systems, life situations, value systems, and literary styles.

The title of this collection is a Tshiluba phrase meaning, "Help me to balance/carry this load."

Davies, Miranda, comp. *Third World, Second Sex: Women's Struggles and National Liberation.* **London: Zed Books, 1983. $10.25. Photographs, illustrations, recommended readings, list of women's organizations. Available in the United States from the Biblio Distribution Center (Totowa, N.J.)**

This is a compilation of interviews and articles by women from the Third World — women, writes Miranda Davies, who "share no one single approach to women's liberation, but [who] show the revolutionary emergence of a new feminist consciousness amongst women in the Third World."

"By revealing the deep-rooted similarities," Ms. Davies writes, "as well as some of the many differences between women's struggles in the West and in the Third World, the . . . collection aims to help build some of the links needed for the development of women's liberation on a truly international scale."

Articles are divided into these categories: women, politics, and organization; role of women in national liberation movements; experience of armed struggle (Zimbabwe, Eritrea, Oman); after the revolution (Mozambique, South Yemen, Iran, Grenada, Nicaragua); autonomous women's movements; struggle against violence; women and health; and women workers fight back (South Korea, Peru, Sri Lanka, India).

Ms. Davies is preparing a second, complementary volume to *Third World, Second Sex.*

Eisen, Arlene. *Women and Revolution in Viet Nam.* **London: Zed Books, 1984. 294pp. $9.95. Recommended reading list, photographs, maps, notes, glossary, list of resources, chronology. Available in the United States from Biblio Distribution Center (Totowa, N.J.).**

In this sequel to a book she wrote in the waning years of U.S. intervention in Vietnam (*Women of Vietnam* [San Francisco: Peoples Press, 1974]), Arlene Eisen offers a frank and unromantic assessment of the personal and societal situation of Vietnamese women since liberation in 1975.

"After the war with the United States ended," Eisen asks, "what happened in Viet Nam? What is the experience of women living in the southern provinces, once occupied by U.S. troops, now building a socialist society? How do they organize for change? How do women who once identified with the U.S. troops they serviced transform their consciousness and recover their dignity? How does the Vietnamese experience compare with the experience of women facing wartime conditions without socialism? Or of women in colonizer, rather than colonized, countries?"

Women and Revolution situates these questions in the historical context of Vietnamese feudalism and patriarchy, French colonialism, and U.S. military aggression. Then, combining numerous interviews and her own historical research, the author presents facts about virtually all aspects of the lives of women in present-day Vietnam with the hope that this information will "illuminate an ongoing discussion" of these and many other questions related to women's liberation and socialism."

Goodwin, June. *Cry Amandla! South African Women and the Question of Power.* **New York: Holmes & Meier, 1985. 253pp. $14.50. Photographs, index, appendixes.**

June Goodwin, a journalist with over fifteen years with National Public Radio, Reuters, and *The Christian Science Monitor*, lived in South Africa from June 1976 to January 1979. Before being permanently based in Johannesburg, she traveled around the country for eight months.

Cry Amandla! is the chronicle of Goodwin's travels—her record of interviews with women on both ends of the political spectrum: black Africans (the majority) and white Afrikaners (descendants of the Dutch settlers; a minority).

"I spoke to men and women," she writes, "but I wrote about the women. They were representative of more than themselves and close to the heart of the society."

Goodwin formed a particularly close friendship with Thenjie Mtintso, a black woman that she calls "the heroine of this book." Thenjie, as her friends call her, was born in the township of Soweto two years before the 1948 implementation of apartheid. "So, like her son, who was born in 1973," Goodwin writes, "she has known nothing but a system of white rule that is deplored throughout the world and called a 'crime against humanity' by the United Nations." Goodwin sees black South Africa and black yearnings for *amandla* (power) through the eyes of this dedicated and passionate woman.

She also examines white perspectives on apartheid. "It was imperative for me to show the Afrikaner women's points of view," she writes, "because they are the wives, sisters, and daughters of the men who invented apartheid and who now rule. It is a society content to be male dominated. But the Afrikaner women are not without responsibility for apartheid. They, like the men, gain materially from its continuation. Interviews with these women show what Thenjie is up against and reveal how the whites can cling to racist views and policies so roundly condemned by the rest of the world."

The two appendixes present documents detailing Thenjie's "banning" and a twenty-five-page facsimile of a pamphlet written in 1978/79 by "wives of members of the Cabinet" explaining that "[white] women are the indispensable 'soldiers' within the country's borders and their spiritual power is South Africa's invisible weapon."

Jordan, June. *On Call: Political Essays.* **Boston: South End Press, 1985. 156pp. $8. Notes, references.**

"From Phillis Wheatley to Walt Whitman, from Stony Brook to Lebanon," writes poet/activist/educator June Jordan, "these writings document my political efforts to coherently fathom all of my universe, and to arrive at a moral judgment that will determine my further political conduct." Except for the opening essay (written in 1979), Jordan explains, "this collection brings together the political writings that the past four years [1981–85] have caused me to produce."

Jordan's powerful and colorful writings deal with a variety of subjects concerning the world that she chooses to call the "First World." "Given that they were the first to exist on the planet," she explains, "and currently make up the majority, the author will refer to that part of the population usually termed Third World as the First World." She writes about Nicaragua, South Africa, and Lebanon, as well as about black North Americans.

Khaing, Mi Mi. *The World of Burmese Women*. London: Zed Books, 1984. 198pp. $12.25. Photographs, statistical tables, bibliography, glossary. Available in the United States from Biblio Distribution Center (Totowa, N.J.).

Mi Mi Khaing, a well-known Burmese writer and social scientist, sets herself the ambitious task of covering in this one book "all aspects of women's participation in the society of one small country [Burma]." Her reasons for undertaking this case study are twofold: first, because "less has been written about Burmese women in post-Independence years than about women in other parts of the world" and, second, because "when all over the world, this century has seen changes in the status of women, particularly with regard to social life, the control and disposal of property, marriage, etc., no such change has been visible in the lives of Burmese women." In Burma, Khaing states forthrightly, "there has been no feminist movement of note." And this in spite of the fact that "Burmese women have not lacked the power to protest or demonstrate either in the past or now."

Khaing blends national pride, scholarly discipline, and personal warmth and commitment in her search for the reasons why Burmese women appear to be content with "life in Burma with its cultural richness, its Burmese food, the leisurely tempo, warmth of friends, and access to pagodas." True, in many ways their societal roles are equal to those of men. True also, they have remained relatively untouched by Western ideas of materialism and individualism. But Khaing's investigation of women in Burmese history, in the family of today, in urban and rural professions, at home, in religion, and in all other facets of their lives demonstrates that there are inequities and there are challenges to traditional values being voiced.

Kishwar, Madhu, and Ruth Vanita, eds. *In Search of Answers: Indian Women's Voices from Manushi*. London: Zed Books, 1984. 312pp. $10.75. Map, photographs, tables, illustrations.

In Search of Answers is an anthology of articles, editorials, and letters to the editor from the first five years of the influential Indian women's journal *Manushi*.

The editors acknowledge the difficulty of generalizing about the life and struggles of Indian women: "Vast differences distinguish the life of women in different parts of the country and within different caste, class, religious, and ethnic groups." This book, they write, "can offer no more than glimpses of the vast, complex, and unplumbed reality of the day to day struggles of millions of ordinary women in India, as well as of some of the few intense moments of organized struggle that managed to get known outside the local area affected."

Articles are grouped under these headings: women's lives; women's struggles; and violence against women (caste and class violence, police violence, and family violence). A selection of five editorials appears in a chapter on women's politics.

Madhu Kishwar's forty-seven-page introduction describes in detail the "continuing struggle" of Indian women, especially rural women, and sets forth sixteen "suggestions" for action. "If our aim is to bring about structural changes," she writes, "our slogan should be not just 'More rights for women' but 'We will leave no basis for power which oppresses women' and 'Human rights equal women's rights.' We must direct our effort in a way that certain basic human rights become non-alienable and non-negotiable, and become the very basis on which all other changes are made."

The concluding chapter provides revealing insights into the aims, aspirations, and day-to-day operations of *Manushi* itself.

Meulenbelt, Anja, Joyce Outshoorn, Selma Sevenhuijsen, and Petra de Vries, eds. *A Creative Tension. Key Issues of Socialist-Feminism: An International Perspective.* **Boston: South End Press, 1984. 152pp. $8.50. Notes.**

This short book brings together six essays that appeared originally in the Netherlands in the magazine *Socialist Feminist Texts.* Articles were chosen for their international scope. They examine the tensions between public and private life, theory and practice, socialism and feminism, production and reproduction, and more.

The concluding essay, "Women's Struggles in the Third World," examines the historical development and present conditions of women in the Third World, analyses the differences in the situations of Third World and Western women, and describes how women in the Third World are fighting for their own liberation in the context of national struggles against foreign domination. Finally, the authors suggest ways in which the members of the women's movement in the West can support the struggles of their sisters in the Third World.

A Creative Tension is international in two respects: (1) it summarizes the development of socialist-feminism in one European country, the Netherlands; and (2) it describes the tensions that activist Dutch women have had to deal with in broadening their perspectives to include consideration of women in the Third World.

Nash, June, and Maria Patricia Fernandez-Kelly, eds. *Women, Men, and the International Division of Labor.* **Albany, N.Y.: State University of New York Press, 1983. 464pp. $14.95. References, statistical tables, notes, index.**

Part of the SUNY series on the anthropology of work, this book examines in its eighteen varied articles the "emerging contradictions in the new international division of labor." The editors note that gender plays a distinct role in these contradictions, and that, just as in the Industrial Revolution in England and Europe during the nineteenth century, young women and children — in developing countries this time around — are the prime labor force because they are the "lowest paid segment of those countries paying the lowest wages."

The book is divided into four sections, each of which contains one or more articles focusing specifically on Third World women. The first section presents an overview of the global economy as it has developed over the past thirty years; the second deals with problems of "production, reproduction, and the household economy"; the third addresses the implications that shifts in industrialization have for migration; and the last section consists of case studies from the U.S. Silicon Valley, the Caribbean, Taiwan, Malaysia, and Southeast Asia in general. The case studies all pertain either to the electronics or the textiles industries, both of which have historically used women in dead-end, low-paying jobs.

This book appears to be a scholarly study, with its charts, notes, and list of eminent contributors, but these actually create and enhance a readable and engrossing presentation of a timely topic.

Nash, June, and Helen Safa, eds. *Women and Change in Latin America: New Directions in Sex and Class.* **South Hadley, Mass.: Bergin & Garvey, 1986. 372pp. $14.95. Notes, tables, photographs, references, index.**

Following on an earlier volume compiled by the same editors (*Sex and Class in Latin America* [South Hadley, Mass.: J. F. Bergin Publishers, 1976]), this collection illustrates how scholars have moved beyond the "descriptive phase" of documenting the contribution women have made to family and society and are now concerned to use women's contributions "as leverage for change in Latin America."

The contributors to this anthology describe the struggles of peasant and market women in the Andes; of female factory workers in Brazil, Mexico, Puerto Rico, and Jamaica; of Colombian women in New York; and of women in the Cuban revolution. They do so in order to inject "gender differences" into the ongoing study and discussion of Latin America's political and economic realities.

To open the book Nash provides a lengthy survey of the research on women in Latin America between 1975 and 1985 and Neuma Aguiar follows with research guidelines for studying women's work in Latin America. The remaining articles are grouped under these headings: "Production for the Market, Social Reproduction, and Biological Reproduction" (chapter 2); "The Articulation of Modes of Production in Industrial and Agricultural Change" (chapter 3); "Migration, Social Reproduction, and Production" (chapter 4); and "Political Action and the State" (chapter 5).

The lists of references cited are helpful for further study. Biographical details on the contributors would have been of interest.

Oboler, Regina Smith. *Women, Power, and Economic Change: The Nandi of Kenya.* Stanford, Calif.: Stanford University Press, 1985. 348pp. $38.50. Cloth. Glossary, tables, photographs, references, index.

"I present here," writes the author, "a case study of the impact of colonialism, capitalism, and a cash economy on sex and gender roles among the Nandi, a semipastoral and patrilineal people of western Kenya. The analysis will focus particularly on the roles of women and men in production, and on women's and men's respective relations to property. Since the sex roles associated with production and property relations are intrinsically connected with sex roles in other areas—in the marriage system, husband-wife relations, kinship, cultural ideals of male and female, ritual relations, participation in community affairs—these areas will also be dealt with where appropriate. Ultimately such an analysis leads to, as it to a large extent grows out of, a desire to know whether the changes that have occurred within Nandi society have been favorable or unfavorable to women. Has women's economic position improved or declined as a result of colonialism and socio-economic change? Is Nandi society marked by a greater or lesser degree of sexual stratification now than it was in the precolonial period?"

Oboler's anthropological fieldwork in the Nandi district in western Kenya from April 1976 to December 1977 equips her to offer well-documented answers to these—and many other—questions about women in traditional societies. Though *Women, Power, and Economic Change* is a reworked doctoral dissertation, the fascinating circumstances of the Nandi people and the author's eye for colorful details keep the book interesting throughout.

Organization of Angolan Women. *Angolan Women Building the Future: From National Liberation to Women's Emancipation.* Trans. Marga Holness. London and Luanda: Zed Press and Organization of Angolan Women, 1984. 152pp. $9.25. Abbreviations list, documents, photographs, statistical tables. Available in the United States from Biblio Distribution Center (Totowa, N.J.).

"African societies in the twentieth century," writes the translator of this collection of conference documents, "are faced with the need to cover, in as short a space of time as possible, a historical trajectory comparable to that covered by Europe since the start of its industrial revolution." The role of women in this accelerated development is the subject of this book.

Eight years after its members helped rid Angola of Portuguese colonial rule the Organization of Angolan Women organized its first congress to take stock of its history and work, to study the present conditions of women in post-colonial reconstruction, and to determine their role in the future development of Angola. While justly proud of the commitment to equality enshrined in Angola's constitution and labor legislation, participants at the congress recognized that the war against machismo, male prejudice, and outmoded traditions was far from won.

The conference reports, speeches, and documents in this volume cover a wide range of topics: brideprice and polygamy, double work, contraception and abortion, socialist family codes, and the relationship between the liberation of women and the struggle to build a socialist nation.

Randall, Margaret. *Women in Cuba: Twenty Years Later.* **Photographs by Judy Janda. Brooklyn, N.Y.: Smyrna Press, 1981. 168pp. $7.95. Tables, photographs, bibliography, appendixes.**

Internationally renowned poet, editor, translator, author, and publisher Margaret Randall lived and worked in Havana from 1969 to 1981 and has written a number of works on Cuba and on the role of women in Cuban society. This book includes seven essays covering such topics as the relationship between feminism and socialism, reproductive rights, the struggle against sexism, the family, and peasant women.

In Cuba, Michele Gibbs Russell writes in the introduction, "state power has already been seized from bourgeois capitalist interests." "Thus," she continues, "the social revolution of a society newly mobilized and deliberately reconstructing itself from the ground up according to political, democratic and economically socialist principles is the context informing the course of women's development and liberation."

"Margaret Randall's survey of Cuba's present-day realities and her understanding of the developmental road women have been traveling since the revolution," Russell writes, "reinforce, above all, the conviction that the simultaneous struggle for bread and roses is the most demanding and potentially explosive process to which any society can be wedded."

Statistics in *Women in Cuba* are current through 1980.

Robertson, Claire, and Iris Berger, eds. *Women and Class in Africa.* **New York: Holmes & Meier, 1985. 300pp. $32.50. Cloth.**

This book is viewed by its editors as "a part of an ongoing effort at reconceptualization [of class so as to include women] and as a contribution that will expand the discussion of women and class into a cultural area that has been on the periphery of current theoretical dialogue in North America. . . . By using gender and class as a unifying theme, these essays will illuminate new facets of African social, economic, and political structures."

Several survey articles deal with the topic of women and class in the African continent as a whole; others deal particularly with Kenya, Ghana, Nigeria, South Africa, Uganda, Zambia, and Zaire.

The contributors to this book are eminently qualified to write on the topic, and the collection is a valuable resource for women's studies or African studies specialists.

Sheridan, Mary, and Janet W. Salaff, eds. *Lives: Chinese Working Women.* **Bloomington, Ind.: Indiana University Press, 1984. 258pp. $8.95. Notes.**

Using the "life history" research method (a blending of history and biography) the writers in this anthology present vivid and intimate portrayals of the life and work of women in Hongkong, Taiwan, and the People's Republic of China.

After an introduction to the subject and to the life history method the editors divide their study into three sections: (1) the lives of the older generation in pre-1949 China, (2) the lives of younger women in Hongkong and Taiwan, and (3) the lives of women in revolution and reconstruction in modern-day China.

Lives introduces the reader to a Hakka stevedore and a revolutionary hero in pre-liberation China, a waitress and a garment worker in Hongkong, an electronics worker in Taiwan, and a pigsty keeper in today's China.

As diverse as the portraits are, they share common themes: the responsibilities of eldest daughters, violence in the family, sibling affection and rivalry, and the primacy of men in private affairs. Other lesser themes also surface: moral regulations and personal codes, loyalty, self-interest, sacrifice, and the importance of food and diet.

Siu, Bobby. *Women of China: Imperialism and Women's Resistance, 1900-1949.* London: Zed Books, 1983. 130pp. $7.50. Tables, statistical appendixes, notes, bibliography, index. Available in the United States from Biblio Distribution Center (Totowa, N.J.).

Much has been written on women in China after 1949. Bobby Siu's work is unique in its analysis of the role of Chinese women in resistance and revolution prior to liberation in 1949.

The author focuses on the first half of the twentieth century for two reasons: (1) because it was during that period that the women's movement emerged and developed as an organized and coordinated historical force, and (2) because that period was such a time of transition for China: from a colonial-feudal-capitalist society to a socialist one.

The author, who holds a doctorate in sociology, defines her tasks in *Women of China* as showing the links between imperialism and the Chinese women's struggle, giving a systematic account of women's role in social change, and illustrating the interrelationship between repression and struggle. *Women of China* opens with a description of imperialism and its effects on China's economy, then focuses on the impact of imperialism on women, and, finally, describes the modes of women's resistance.

"The central thesis of this book," writes Dr. Siu, "is that the resistance movements of working-class and peasant women in China sprang from the encroachment of imperialism upon China, and that the women who participated in these movements played an important role in its removal." Her final chapter summarizes the lessons to be learned from the history of women's resistance in China: (1) women *were* agents of social change; (2) the oppression and exploitation of women were eliminated through effective organization and mobilization by the women themselves; (3) class is stronger than gender in the mobilization process, and (4) government attempts to repress and "institutionalize" the women's movement—i.e., to suppress the radicals and co-opt the moderates—failed in China and is destined to fail in other Third World countries as well.

"As long as the structural sources of women's discontent remain," Siu concludes, "and [as long as] only certain women benefit from the government's institutional changes—as was the case of China before 1949—the women's movement will continue."

Son Dug-Soo, and Lee Mi-Kyung. *My Mother's Name Is Worry: A Preliminary Report of the Study on Poor Women in Korea.* **Seoul: Christian Institute for the Study of Justice and Development, 1983. 154pp. $5. Charts, statistical tables.**

My Mother's Name describes the influence of Korea's economic development policies in the 1960s and 1970s on poor women of urban and rural areas. Industrial workers are not included because—the authors state—there are other studies on this question in Korea.

"The poor women in Korea," write two directors of the Christian Institute, "constitute the core of the *Minjung* (bottom) of the Korean society. This study of poor women is an exposure of the depth of dehumanization in the process of the so-called economic growth or modernization in Korea."

The authors, one (Son) a professor at Ewha Woman's University and the other (Lee) a researcher at the Christian Institute, introduce their study by writing that "concern for the problems of women and the direction of the women's movement must not be limited simply to the question of sexual discrimination and the relative position of men and women." "Such an approach," they continue, "is simply a middle and upper class movement of advanced or developed nations."

"Women from the poor class," Son and Lee explain, "are doubly discriminated against, first as poor, and secondly as women within that depressed group." For this reason, they conclude, "women within the Third World, and Korea, must take part in the movement for the liberation of women, from the viewpoint of poor women."

This survey combines statistical data and thirteen gripping case histories of Korean women's struggles in rural and urban poverty.

Swantz, Marja-Liisa. *Women in Development: A Creative Role Denied?* **London: C. Hurst, 1985. 178pp. $11.95. Map, bibliography, index. Available in the United States from St. Martin's Press (New York).**

"In the Tanzanian press and at public meetings," writes the author of this detailed field study, "women are exhorted to become part of the country's development." The thinking behind these exhortations, Swantz believes, is that "women have remained onlookers who have to be told to participate and to work harder in the process of development. It is assumed that what is lacking is the knowledge and the desire to share dynamically in the process of building a new society."

"In reality," writes the author, "it is the women who, in their own persons, integrate the new development with the old." *Women in Development* demonstrates how the two essential sectors of Tanzania's national life, agricultural production and the nurture of children, "are in the hands of women, while the men, writing in newspapers, and addressing the women from platforms, urge them to 'take part in development.'"

Now the director of the Institute of Development Studies at the University of Helsinki, Finland, Dr. Swantz was a university research fellow in Tanzania in the early 1970s and later codirected a participatory research project in Tanzania for four years.

Tawil, Raymonda Hawa. *My Home, My Prison.* **London: Zed Books, 1983. 266pp. $7.50. Postscript, epilogue. Available in the United States from Biblio Distribution Center (Totowa, N.J.).**

Raymonda Tawil, a Palestinian journalist, wrote this gripping account of her life during one of her periods of house arrest. From the start, with the author's exchange with an Israeli woman soldier as she waits in the military governor's office, the book deals with questions of women's equality as much as with equality among Israelis, Jordanians, and Palestinians. The military governor announces the fact of her house arrest. "Like all Palestinians," Tawil writes, "I will bear my prison with me in my heart wherever I go. As a woman, I will suffer a double alienation." She vows to "record the story of all my prisons, all my walls . . ."

Permeating Tawil's life story is the impressive figure of her activist mother, a Palestinian who was born in the United States but who lived her adult life as an Arab patriot in the land of her ancestors. As the mother lived, so lives the daughter, fearlessly struggling in a complicated and violent society.

Tawil knows that throughout her whole life she has been denied her freedom "in many ways: as a Palestinian, belonging to a people deprived of rights and dignity; as a woman in a semifeudal, patriarchal society; as a citizen of a territory under foreign military occupation; as an individual in a traditionalist, oppressive environment that restricts individual liberties." Her story is of isolation, silence, confinement, intimidation, and harassment, but also of solidarity, outspokenness, freedom, fearlessness, and small victories for truth. Reading it is to encounter almost personally these many experiences.

Webster, John C. B., and Ellen Low Webster, eds. *The Church and Women in the Third World.* **Philadelphia: Westminster, 1985. 168pp. $11.95. Notes, tables, bibliography.**

"Although much is being written about Third World churches and Third World women," state the editors, "the scholarly literature linking the two is surprisingly meager." The Websters, veteran missionaries in India, aim to fill this void with this anthology of essays on Christian images of women, the role of women in the church, and the church and the status of women.

Specific topics include images of Chinese women (by Shirley Garrett), Catholic women of India (by Stella Faria), coming-of-age in a Latin church (by Katherine Gilfeather), the role of women in Africa's new religions (by Bennetta Jules-Rosette), assumptions about Indian women underlying Protestant church policies and programs (by John Webster), and women in Philippine "basic Christian communities" (by Mark Ratkus).

Ellen Low Webster's concluding annotated bibliography of "recent empirical studies" on the church and women in the Third World is a major contribution to ongoing studies in this vital field. "Women in most Third World countries," Webster writes, "have been impacted in a variety of ways by Christianity, a fact many researchers on women tend to overlook." "In like manner," she continues, "researchers who have written about churches in the Third World often ignore the fact that women comprise half the churches' membership and have helped make the churches what they are today."

Webster's survey of the literature reveals that scholarly works that link the two subjects ('church' and 'women') are "sparse, difficult to find, and limited almost exclusively to article- rather than book-length studies." The "frequent and artificial separation" of the subjects is due, she suspects, to "a shared assumption that the church is a male preserve unrelated to women."

The bibliography contains forty-six annotated entries divided into three regional sections: Africa, Asia, and Latin America.

Wolf, Margery. *Revolution Postponed: Women in Contemporary China.* **Stanford, Calif.: Stanford University Press, 1985. 286pp. $24.95. Cloth. Tables, notes, index.**

Based on nearly a year of field research and interviews with over three hundred women in six widely separated rural and urban areas, *Revolution Postponed* presents a vivid picture of Chinese women today—their day-to-day lives, their views of the present, and their hopes for the future.

To date, Wolf contends, nothing approximating equality has been achieved: in working conditions, in pay, in educational opportunity. Wolf's study demonstrates that in the cities, and to a lesser extent in the countryside, women are better off than in prerevolutionary China. But nowhere except in "the rhetoric of the regime," she says, are they equal to men.

If the liberation of women in China is to truly succeed, Wolf believes, Chinese feminists "must be allowed to do as Mao did, to gather together like-minded people who see the shortcomings of the present social order and want to change it. Everything I read and hear suggests that those people are out there, but thus far they are isolated souls only partially aware of their shared oppression. Until they join together, they are not a movement, let alone a revolution."

Margery Wolf is the author of *House of Lim* (1968) and *The Family in Rural Taiwan* (1972).

***Women in Nigeria Today.* London: Zed Books, 1985. 258pp. $9.95. Notes on contributors, tables, statistical tables, notes, references, index. Available in the United States from Biblio Distribution Center (Totowa, N.J.).**

Is the oppression of women an aspect of, and subordinate to, class oppression? Or should the struggle against women's oppression be conducted in alliance with the struggle against class oppression, but with recognition given to and action taken on the particular ways in which women are oppressed? "On-going, somewhat acrimonious" debates among faculty members at Nigeria's Ahmadu Bello University about these critical issues of the worldwide women's movement resulted in a seminar at the university in May 1982 on the subject of women in Nigeria today.

In two days of study, conference participants from a variety of backgrounds and from all parts of the country concluded that women in Nigeria are considered socially subordinate to men because of their biological difference and that they are oppressed simply because they are women. The majority of participants reportedly agreed that the conclusion most relevant in understanding the position of women in Nigeria today was that class exploitation and gender subordination interact with each other to define women's position in society.

The twenty-three conference papers collected in this volume explore theoretical perspectives, as well as the history and contemporary experiences of urban and rural women in Nigeria. Each section contains a helpful "rapporteur's summary."

Conference participants formed an organization, Women in Nigeria, to engage in research, policy-making, dissemination of information, and action aimed at improving the conditions of women.

Bibliographies

Ballou, Patricia K. *Women: A Bibliography of Bibliographies.* **Boston: G. K. Hall, 1980. 156pp.**

Pages 30–41 in this bibliography contain forty-two annotated entries dealing with the Third World (general), Latin America, Middle East, and Asia. All of the bibliographies were published in the 1970s.

Byrne, Pamela R., and Suzanne R. Ontiveros, eds. *Women in the Third World: A Historical Bibliography.* **Santa Barbara, Calif. and Oxford: ABC-Clio, 1986. 152pp. Subject and author indexes.**

This research guide is one in ABC-Clio's "new generation of annotated bibliographies that provide comprehensive control of the recent journal literature on high-interest topics in history and the related social sciences." Earlier guides in this series — both edited by Lynne B. Iglitzin and Ruth Ross — were *Women in the World: A Comparative Study* (1976) and *Women in the World, 1975–1985: The Women's Decade* (1985, 2nd rev. ed.).

Women in the Third World contains 601 abstracts and citations of journal articles drawn from a database of over 2,000 periodicals published in some ninety countries. All the entries in this volume were published between 1970 and 1985.

Entries are arranged alphabetically by author and categorized into one general and six regional chapters.

Caughman, Susan. *Women and Development in Mali: An Annotated Bibliography.* **Bibliography Series No. 6. Addis Ababa: UN Economic**

Commission for Africa, African Training and Research Centre for Women. 34pp.

Cheng, Lucie, Charlotte Furth, and Hon-ming Yip. *Women in China: Bibliography of Available English Language Materials.* Berkeley, Calif.: University of California, Center for Chinese Studies, Institute of East Asian Studies, 1984. 109pp. $12. List of sources surveyed, index of Chinese women as subjects, author index.

Women in China contains 4,107 entries, current to the summer of 1981. Materials selected from over 250 journals and almost one hundred bibliographies are classified under twelve general headings and eighty-seven subheadings. General headings are: education; emancipation movements; health and population; labor and production; literature; art and folklore; marriage and the family; politics and the law; psychology and religion; science, technology and the military; sport and fashion; and Western women in China. Few of the entries are annotated.

The editors highlight two particularly important categories of published material included in *Women in China*. These are: (1) "imaginative literature," such as novels, poetry, and plays by or about women; and (2) news and opinion articles translated from the post-1950 Chinese press by—among others—the U.S. government-sponsored Joint Publications Research Service.

Fan Kok Sim. *Women in Southeast Asia: A Bibliography.* Boston: G. K. Hall Reference Books, 1982. 446pp. $55.

International Women's Tribune Centre. *Bibliography of Documentation Prepared for [United Nations] Decade Conferences.* (June 1984 edition of *The Tribune* [English and Spanish]). New York: International Women's Tribune Centre. 22pp. $2.

Koh, Hesung Chung, et al. *Korean and Japanese Women: An Analytic Bibliographical Guide.* Westport, Conn.: Greenwood Press, 1982. 904pp. $65.

Lytle, Elizabeth. *Women in India: A Comprehensive Bibliography.* Public Administration Series No. P109. Monticello, Ill.: Vance Bibliographies, 1978. 29pp.

McKay, Nellie. *Twentieth Century Third World Women Writers, Black American and African: Selected Bibliography.* Madison: University of Wisconsin System, Women's Studies Librarian-at-Large, 1983.

Marshall, Marion, comp. *Selected Bibliography of Women in the Arab World with Particular Emphasis on Morocco.* Minneapolis.: University of Minnesota, Women and International Development Research and Information Center, 1983. 13pp.

Mascarenhas, Ophelia, and Marjorie Mbilinyi. *Women in Tanzania: An Analytical Bibliography.* New York: Holmes and Meier, 1985. 256pp. $29.50.

Moghdessian, Samira, comp. *The Status of the Arab Woman: A Selected Bibliography.* London: Mansell Publishing House, 1980.

Muchena, Olivia, ed. *Women and Development in Zimbabwe: An Annotated Bibliography.* Bibliography Series No. 9. Addis Ababa: UN

Economic Commission for Africa, African Training and Research Centre for Women, 1984. 50pp.

Phillips, Beverly R., comp. and ed. *Women in Rural Development: A Bibliography.* Training and Methods Series No. 29. Supplement. Madison: University of Wisconsin–Madison, Land Tenure Center, April 1982. 45pp.

Entries are divided into these geographical categories: general; Africa; Asia; Europe; Latin America; Near East; New Zealand; and the United States. Each item contains one or more keyword descriptors.

al-Qazzaz, Ayad. *Women in the Middle East and North Africa: An Annotated Bibliography.* Middle East Monographs No. 2. Austin: University of Texas, Center for Middle Eastern Studies, 1977. 178pp. Indexes (country and subject).

Entries of English-language materials are arranged in alphabetical order with none more recent than 1976.

Raccagni, Michelle. *The Modern Arab Woman: A Bibliography.* Metuchen, N.J.: Scarecrow Press, 1978. 272pp. Indexes (author and subject).

This comprehensive collection of three thousand titles contains "all books, articles, reports and dissertations in Western languages, principally English and French, as well as Arabic" on the situation of Arab women during the last 150 years. Entries are arranged by subject and then by country (with topical subdivisions). The bibliography is sparsely annotated.

Sakala, Carol. *Women of South Asia: A Guide to Resources.* Millwood, N.Y.: Kraus International, 1980. 517pp. $40.

Saulniers, Suzanne Smith, and Cathy A. Rakowski. *Women in the Development Process: A Select Bibliography on Women in Sub-Saharan Africa and Latin America.* Austin: University of Texas, Institute of Latin American Studies, 1977. 287pp.

Searing, Susan. *Women and Politics in Latin America: A Selective Bibliography.* Madison: University of Wisconsin System, Women's Studies Librarian-at-Large, 1984.

_____.*Women and Power: A Bibliography of Feminist Writings.* Madison: University of Wisconsin System, Women's Studies Librarian-at-Large, 1983.

Wei, Karen T., comp. *Women in China.* Bibliographies and Indexes in Women's Studies No.1. Westport, Conn.: Greenwood Press, 1984. 250pp. $35.

White, Karen. *Women in Development: An Annotated Bibliography for the World Bank.* Washington, D.C.: International Center for Research on Women, June 1985. 39pp. Index (geographical).

The 110 items in this bibliography are arranged in these subject categories: general; agriculture and rural development; water and sanitation; housing and urban services; education and training; small-scale enterprise; energy; health and nutrition; and transportation. References are to articles from books and periodicals.

Williamson, Jane. *New Feminist Scholarship: A Guide to Bibliographies.* **Westbury, N.Y.: Feminist Press, 1979. List of publishers, indexes (author and title).**

New Feminist Scholarship refers readers to 391 bibliographies, resource lists, and literary reviews that were published separately or that appeared as periodical articles. All are in English, though not necessarily of U.S. origin. Chapters are devoted to Third World countries (12 items) and women and development (8 items). Approximately one-half of the entries are annotated.

Catalogs, Directories, Guides

Allen, Martha Leslie. *Index/Directory of Women's Media.* **Washington, D.C.: Women's Institute for Freedom of the Press, 1986. $12.**

This annual directory includes descriptive lists of women's periodicals, news services, film groups, distributors, bookstores, and much more. Entries are national and international.

Hansen, Lynn, and Maria Riley, O.P., comp. *Women Workers' Resource Directory.* **Washington, D.C.: Center of Concern, August 1985. 51pp.**

Resources in this directory are arranged in four categories: topics of interest (e.g., industrial health hazards, church involvement with labor issues); industries; international labor activities; and regions (Americas, Asia, Europe). Contents include organizations, books, periodicals, articles, and occasional papers.

Isis International. *Women in Development: A Resource Guide for Organization and Action.* **Rome: Isis International, 1983. 226pp. $12. Photographs, illustrations, notes.**

This indispensable guide to resources on women in development focuses on these critical issues: multinationals; rural development and food production, including appropriate technology and income generation; health; education and communication; and migration and tourism.

Each chapter begins with one or more well-documented overview articles. The "Resources for Research and Organizing" portion of each of the five chapters contains extensively annotated lists of organizations, books, periodicals, bibliographies, pamphlets, and articles.

Vaid, Jyotsna, Barbara Miller, and Janice Hyde, eds. *South Asian Women at Home and Abroad: A Guide to Resources.* **La Jolla, Calif.: Committee on South Asian Women, 1984. 90pp. $7.**

Vavrus, Linda Gire, with Ron Cadieux and the staff of the Non-Formal Education Information Center. *Women in Development: A Selected Annotated Bibliography and Resource Guide.* **East Lansing, Mich.: Non-Formal Education Information Center, Michigan State University, College of Education, 1980. 70pp. $5.**

This annotated bibliography on the subject of women in development is compiled from the resource collection of the NFE Information Center. Interest in this subject, say the editors, "is characterized by a common concern for the dynamic situation of women interacting with changing socioeconomic conditions and processes. Special focus is found on the changing statuses, roles, relationships, and opportunities of poor women, particularly as these are affected by development policies and practices."

The guide includes books (categorized by topic and region), journals and periodicals, bibliographies, organizations, and recent acquisitions. Subject headings in the books section are: general development; agriculture and food production; education; employment and work; and family, nutrition, and health.

Study Guides and Curriculum Materials

Case, Patricia J., ed. and comp. *Field Guide to Alternative Media: A Directory to Reference and Selection Tools Useful in Accessing Small and Alternative Press Publications and Independently Produced Media.* **Chicago: Task Force on Alternatives in Print, Social Responsibilities Round Table, American Library Association, 1984. 44pp. $6. Distributed by the Office of Library Outreach Services, c/o ALA, 50 E. Huron St., Chicago, IL 60611. Bibliography, index.**

This excellent guide contains annotated listings of more than 160 "tools that list, index, or review primarily small and alternative press publications and independently produced media." The guide is divided into four sections: subject and trade directories; indices and subject bibliographies; trade and review media; and bookstore and distributor catalogs. The *Field Guide* describes twenty alternative resources specifically on women, including bookstores, periodicals, and books.

Global Women's History. **St. Louis Park, Minn.: Glenhurst Publications, 1985.**

This secondary to adult curriculum includes books, teacher's guides, sound filmstrips, and computer software. Write for brochure.

In Search of Our Past. **Newton, Mass.: Education Development Center, 1980.**

This looseleaf curriculum unit was prepared by the Women's Studies Program of the Berkeley Unified School District (Berkeley, California). The guide, in the words of its compilers, "grew out of the need we saw for a supplemental curriculum about women of different ethnic backgrounds that could be incorporated into existing American History or World History courses at the junior high school level." "Traditional history textbooks," they say, "included little about the history of women, the different peoples of America, non-Western peoples, or the lives of ordinary people as an integral part of history."

The material is divided into three units: "Women under Feudalism in Western Europe and China"; "Women and the Industrial Revolution"; and "Women in Change: Twentieth Century Women in Transition." Each unit contains several sections: unit outline, teacher guide, student materials (includes selected readings), and bibliography. Of particular interest are three topics covered in unit 3 — women and political change: Third World women (China and South Africa); women struggle to consolidate political change (Cuba); and the international women's movement.

Although most of the readings are from publications copyrighted during the 1970s, they are in a sense timeless, dealing as they do with women's history. Because the format is so well thought out, the readings could be updated or replaced by a film or other medium. The units were carefully planned and tested by experienced teachers and could serve as a model for anyone wishing to develop her or his own materials.

Kindervatter, Suzanne. *Women Working Together.* **Washington, D.C.: OEF International, 1983. 100pp. $10.**

Based on work with community-level women's groups in Central America and Thailand, this handbook consists of more than forty proven participatory learning activities. Designed as a resource for field workers, adult educators, extension agents, and group leaders, *Women Working Together* aims to enable women "to organize for a variety of small enterprise and community development efforts."

Learning activities make extensive use of local materials and are adaptable for literate or preliterate groups. The handbook can be used as the basis for a nonformal education program or as a means to increase women's participation in technical training, cooperatives, and other development programs.

Topics include women and work, setting and achieving goals, working as a group, community problem-solving, legal rights, family relationships and finances, and more.

Spanish- and French-language editions are also available ($12 each).

Overseas Education Fund. *Women and World Issues: An Action Handbook for Your Community.* **Washington, D.C.: Overseas Education Fund, 1981. 68pp. $8.**

Based on the experiences of participants in five "Women and World Issues Workshops" held across the United States in 1980–81, this handbook is described as "an ideal resource for people interested in organizing community workshops to learn more about women overseas and how Third World development problems are linked with those in developed nations."

The handbook is divided into three sections: "Setting the Stage"; "'Action' Model and How to Use It"; and "Guide for Task Groups." The educational model is participatory and emphasizes broad-based community involvement.

Social Studies School Service. 1985 Catalog. **Culver City, Calif.: Social Studies School Service, 1985. 274pp. Free.**

This well-designed catalog is a gold mine of educational materials for the social studies teacher. Subject areas include world history and geography, area studies, arms race and nuclear war, global education, and more. Materials include paperbacks, multimedia kits, videocassettes, computer software, reproducible spirit masters, simulations, and a variety of other teaching tools. Each of the items is available directly from the School Service, many of them with quantity discounts.

Sri Lanka Women's Bureau and OEF International. *Navamaga: Training Activities for Group Building, Health, and Income Generation.* **Washington, D.C.: OEF International, 1983. 150pp. $12.**

"Navamaga" means "new path" in Singhalese, one of Sri Lanka's national languages.

This handbook was created by rural Sri Lankan field workers for their colleagues around the world. Its more than sixty training activities — all intended to be used with women's or mixed groups at the village level — cover issues such as group building, decision making and cooperation, leadership, assessing needs, mobilizing local resources, "painless" planning, as well as other practical subjects such as pig-raising and food preservation.

Each technical section on health and income generation includes both a participatory activity and a basic technical information sheet. Guidelines are provided to aid in identifying additional technical expertise at the local level.

French- and Spanish-language editions are also available.

Stanford Program on International and Cross-Cultural Education (SPICE). *Catalogue of Materials.* **Stanford, Calif.: SPICE, 1985. 17pp. Free.**

The aim of SPICE is to use scholarly resources in international studies and education in cooperative endeavors with precollegiate educators to improve international and cross-cultural education at the elementary and secondary levels. The major activities of the program are curriculum development and in-service education. SPICE encompasses five projects at present: China, Japan, Africa, Latin America, and international security and arms control.

This catalog describes the educational materials that SPICE makes available in each of these subject areas.

Staudt, Kathleen. *Women in Development: Courses and Curriculum Integration.* **East Lansing: Michigan State University, 1985. 42pp. $3.50.**

This essay outlines the essential elements of a course in women in development, including suggestions about textbooks, supplementary materials, and projects. It also discusses the integration of a women in development unit into other courses, focusing on development and development administration. Appendixes contain numerous references for instructor preparation and/or assignments, as well as sample course syllabi.

The author is an associate professor of political science and coordinator of women's studies at the University of Texas at El Paso.

Wien, Barbara J., ed. *Peace and World Order Studies: A Curriculum Guide.* **New York: World Policy Institute, 1984. 4th ed. 741pp. $14.95.**

This guide contains over one hundred course syllabi and outlines drawn from a wide variety of disciplines, including political science, literature, international law, and the natural sciences. There are four-teen subject divisions, including human rights and social justice, world political economy and economic justice, and peacemaking and non-violence.

The chapter "Women and World Order" contains five course outlines: (1) "Women, Work, Wealth, and the Third World"; (2) "Sex Roles: Cross Cultural Perspectives"; (3) "Anthropology of Women"; (4) "Women in Politics"; and (5) "Women and Politics." Lists of recom-mended readings are extensive.

In addition to the course outlines, *Peace and World Order Studies* contains a valuable five-part section of resources: funding sources; filmography; periodicals and journals; organizations; and bibliography.

Women and Hunger. **Baltimore, Md.: Church World Service, Office on Global Education, 1985. 18pp.**

This one-hour curriculum is intended for high-school to adult stu-dents who are just beginning to learn about hunger issues. Its objectives are to lead students: "(1) to touch the pain and promise of women's lives in other parts of the world; (2) to recall the biblical mandate for Chris-tian response in the face of suffering, inequity, and injustice; and (3) to know that concerned groups and individuals can make a difference and to grasp what [they] can do.

The manual is well-designed. The CWS Office on Global Education also has attractive supplementary posters and other materials available for use in the study course.

Women in the World. **Berkeley, Calif.: Women in the World, Curricu-lum Resource Project, 1986.**

This handbook is designed to inform educators about available stu-dent materials and resources about women that could be integrated into world history and area studies courses at the secondary-school level. The editors describe the content of each listing and offer suggestions for its use in the classroom. Only those resources that are easily accessible and appropriate for students at the secondary level are included.

Entries are grouped under the following geographical and historical headings: prehistory; Africa Sub-Sahara; North Africa; Middle East; Europe to the Renaissance; Europe through the twentieth century; the Soviet Union; China, Japan, and Korea: Southeast Asia; India; Austra-lia and New Zealand; Latin America; and cross-cultural topics.

Print and nonprint materials are included.

Reference Books

Morgan, Robin, ed. *Sisterhood Is Global: The International Women's Movement Anthology.* **Garden City, N.Y.: Anchor Press/Doubleday, 1984. 815pp. $12.95.**

An ambitious project that took seventeen years to complete, from conception to production, *Sisterhood Is Global* is unique among women's books. It is an anthology, a collection of articles by women from around the world about their local situations, but it is also a reference work, containing statistics and facts pertinent to women in each country covered, and suggestions for further reading and study.

The book is a logical follow-up to the editor's anthology of articles from the U.S. women's movement, *Sisterhood Is Powerful* (1970). Under the headings of seventy countries and the United Nations, arranged alphabetically, information is organized in this way: statistical preface (geographical placement and area description, demography, government, economy, gynography, herstory, and mythography), an article by a woman representative of the country, and suggested further reading.

The editor recognizes the contributions of her many associates ("literally thousands of women around the world"), whose collaboration was essential, and stands somewhat in awe of her own task. "The book you hold in your hands," she writes, "reflects the intense network of contacts and interlocking activities the world's women have built over the past two decades. It reflects the fact that this foundation now is solid enough to support a genuine global movement of women which will have enormous political impact through the end of this century, and will create a transnational transformation in the next century. . . . Just as *Sisterhood Is Global* is a cross-cultural, cross-age-group, cross-occupation/class, cross-racial, cross-sexual-preference, and cross-ideological assemblage of women's voices, so is the movement itself." A necessary reference work for any library and a valuable book for anyone interested in the international women's movement.

Searing, Susan. *New Reference Works in Women's Studies, 1982/83.* Madison: University of Wisconsin System, Women's Studies Librarian-at-Large, 1983.

_____. *New Reference Works in Women's Studies, 1983/84.* Madison: University of Wisconsin System, Women's Studies Librarian-at-Large, 1984.

SUPPLEMENTARY LIST OF BOOKS

THIRD WORLD

Anker, Richard, Mayra Buvinić, and Nadia H. Youssef, eds. *Women's Roles and Population Trends in the Third World.* London: Croom Helm, 1982.

Black, Naomi, and Ann Baker Cottrell, eds. *Women and World Change: Equity Issues in Development.* Beverly Hills, Calif.: Sage Publications, 1981.

Bourguignon, Erika, et al. *A World of Women: Anthropological Studies of Women in the Societies of the World.* New York and London: Praeger Publishers, 1980. 364pp.

Brock-Utne, Birgit. *Educating for Peace: A Feminist Perspective.* New York: Pergamon/Athene Series, 1985. 174pp. $10.95.

Buvinić, Mayra, Margaret A. Lycette, William P. McGreevey, eds. *Women and Poverty in the Third World.* Baltimore: Johns Hopkins University Press, 1983. 344pp. $27.95.

Cambridge Women's Peace Collective. *My Country Is the Whole World.* Boston: Routledge and Kegan Paul, 1984. 306pp. $9.95.

Dauber, Roslyn, and Melinda L. Cain, eds. *Women and Technological Change in Developing Countries.* Boulder, Colo.: Westview Press, 1981. 266pp.

Etienne, Mona, Eleanor Leacock, et al. *Women and Colonization: Anthropological Perspectives.* South Hadley, Mass.: Bergin and Garvey, 1980. 352pp. $12.95.

Farley, Jennie, ed. *Women Workers in Fifteen Countries.* Ithaca, N.Y.: Cornell University, School of Industrial and Labor Relations, 1985. 196pp. $9.95.

Hosken, Fran P. *The Hosken Report: Genital/Sexual Mutilation of Females.* Lexington, Mass.: Women's International Network, 1983. 344pp. $17.

Jayawardena, Kumari. *Feminism and Nationalism in the Third World.* London: Zed Books, 1985. 256pp. $10.75.

Leacock, Eleanor, Helen I. Safa, et al. *Women's Work: Development and the Division of Labor by Gender.* South Hadley, Mass.: Bergin & Garvey, 1986. 304pp. $16.95.

Leahy, Margaret E. *Development Strategies and the Status of Women: A Comparative Study of United States, Mexico, Soviet Union, Cuba.* Boulder, Colo.: Lynne Rienner Publishers, 1986. 168pp. $25. Cloth.

Lindsay, Beverly. *Comparative Perspectives of Third World Women: The Impact of Race, Sex, and Class.* New York: Praeger, United Nations Economic Commission, 1980.

Moraga, Cherríe, and Gloria Anzaldua, eds. *This Bridge Called My Back: Writings by Radical Women of Color.* New York: Kitchen Table: Women of Color Press, 1981. 262pp. $8.95.

Sachs, Carolyn. *The Invisible Farmers: Women in Agricultural Production.* Totowa, N.J.: Rowman and Allanheld, 1984. 138pp. $23.95.

Schipper, Mineke. *Unheard Words: Women and Literature in Africa, the Arab World, Asia, the Caribbean, and Latin America.* London: Allison and Busby, 1985.

Soldon, Norbert C., ed. *The World of Women's Trade Unionism: Comparative Historical Essays.* Westport, Conn.: Greenwood Press, 1985. 256pp. $35. Cloth.

Welch, Sharon D. *Communities of Resistance and Solidarity: A Feminist Theology of Liberation.* Maryknoll, N.Y.: Orbis, 1985. 102pp. $7.95

Women and Development Network of Australia. *Women, Aid & Development.* Sydney: Women and Development Network, 1983. 146pp. $10.

AFRICA

Gadant, Monique, ed. *Women of the Mediterranean.* London: Zed Books, 1986. 240pp. $10.95.

Harrison, Nancy. *Winnie Mandela.* New York: George Braziller, 1986. $14.95. Cloth.

Joseph, Helen. *Side by Side.* London: Zed Books, 1986. 272pp. $10.95.

Lapchick, Richard E., and Stephanie Urdang. *Oppression and Resistance: The Struggle of Women in Southern Africa.* Westport, Conn.: Greenwood Press, 1982. 197pp. $27.50.

Obbo, Christine. *African Women: Their Struggle for Economic Independence.* London: Zed Books, 1980. 166pp. $8.75.

Perold, Helene, and Sached Trust, eds. *Working Women: A Portrait of South Africa's Black Women Workers.* Johannesburg: Ravan Press, 1985. 144pp.

Women under Apartheid: In Photographs and Text. London: International Defence and Aid Fund for Southern Africa, 1981. 120pp.

ASIA AND PACIFIC

Andors, Phyllis. *The Unfinished Liberation of Chinese Women, 1949–1980.* Bloomington, Ind.: Indiana University Press, 1983. 212pp.

Croll, Elisabeth. *Chinese Women since Mao.* White Plains, N.Y.: M. E. Sharpe, 1983.

Fawcett, James T., Siew-Ean Khoo, and Peter C. Smith. *Women in the Cities of Asia: Migration and Urban Adaptation.* Boulder, Colo.: Westview Press, 1984.

Hemmel, Vibeke, and Pia Sindbjerg. *Women in Rural China: Policy towards Women before and after the Cultural Revolution.* Atlantic Highlands, N.J.: Humanities Press, 1984.

Jeffery, Patricia. *Frogs in a Well: Indian Women in Purdah.* London: Zed Books, 1979. 188pp. $9.25.

Johnson, Kay Ann. *Women, the Family, and Peasant Revolution in China.* Chicago: University of Chicago Press, 1984. 260pp. $23.

Kendall, Laurel, and Mark Peterson, eds. *Korean Women: View from the Inner Room.* New Haven, Conn.: East Rock Press, 1984. 208pp.

Liddle, Joanna, and Rama Joshi. *Daughters of Independence: Gender, Caste, and Class in India.* London: Zed Books, 1985. 272pp. $9.95.

Majupuria, T.C., and Indra Majupuria. *Nepalese Women.* Kathmandu, Nepal: published by the authors at Tribhuvan University, Kiripur, n.d. 303pp. $8.75.

Mies, Maria. *The Lace Makers of Narsapur: Indian Housewives Produce for the World Market.* London: Zed Books, 1982. 196pp. $9.25.

Omvedt, Gail. *We Will Smash This Prison! Indian Women in Struggle.* London: Zed Books, 1980. 192pp. $6.95.

Sebstad, Jeneffer. *Women and Self-Reliance in India: The SEWA Story.* London: Zed Books, 1985. 272pp. $9.95.

Skjonsberg, Else. *A Special Caste? Tamil Women of Sri Lanka.* London: Zed Books, 1982. 144pp. $8.75.

LATIN AMERICA AND CARIBBEAN

Arrom, Silvia Marina. *The Women of Mexico City, 1790–1857.* Stanford, Calif.: Stanford University Press, 1985. 384pp. $42.50. Cloth.

Bourque, Susan C., and Kay B. Warren. *Women of the Andes: Patriarchy and Social Change in Two Peruvian Towns.* Ann Arbor: University of Michigan Press, 1982.

Deighton, Jane, Cathy Cain, Rossana Horsley, and Sarah Stewart. *Sweet Ramparts: Women in Revolutionary Nicaragua.* London: Nicaragua Solidarity Campaign/War on Want Campaigns, 1983. £2.75. Available from Third World Publications, 151 Stratford Rd., Birmingham B11 1RD, England.

Latin American Women's Collective. *Slaves of Slaves: The Challenge of Latin American Women.* London: Zed Books, 1980. 186pp. $9.25.

Nash, June, Helen Safa, et al. *Sex and Class in Latin America: Women's Perspectives on Economics, Politics, and the Family in the Third World.* South Hadley, Mass.: Bergin and Garvey, 1980. 352pp. $12.95.

Randall, Margaret. *Sandino's Daughters.* Vancouver: New Star Books, 1981. 220pp. $7.95.

Thomson, Marilyn, and Nora Wintour. *Women of El Salvador: The Price of Freedom.* London: Zed Books and War on Want, 1985. 176pp. $9.25.

MIDDLE EAST

Eickelman, Christine. *Women and Community in Oman.* New York: New York University Press, 1985. 240pp. $10.

Fernea, Elizabeth Warnock, ed. *Women and the Family in the Middle East: New Voices of Change.* Austin: University of Texas Press, 1985. 356pp.

Minai, Naila. *Women in Islam.* New York: Seaview Books, 1981.

el Saadawi, Nawal. *The Hidden Face of Eve: Women in the Arab World.* London: Zed Books, 1982. 224pp. $9.25.

Walther, Wiebke. *Woman in Islam.* Totowa, N.J.: Rowman and Allanheld, 1982. 204pp. $35.

INFORMATION SOURCES

For lists of other books on the subject of women in the Third World see the bibliographies, catalogs, and reference books described above (pp. 41–49). The recommended readings at the end of each country chapter in *Sisterhood Is Global* (see p. 48 above) are especially useful.

To keep current on new releases we suggest that you request book catalogs from the publishers represented in this chapter and consult these publications:

New Books on Women & Feminism. Published by Susan Searing, Women's Studies Librarian, University of Wisconsin System, 112A Memorial Library, 728 State St., Madison, WI 53706. 2 issues/year. 28cm. 100pp. Individuals and women's programs: $12/year. Institutional subscription: $24/year.

New Books, say its editors, "has grown to become the fullest readily accessible listing of English-language materials in women's studies." The semi-annual publication contains unannotated lists of books, periodicals, and non-print materials divided into more than twenty-five subject categories (with numerous cross-references). Each title includes all the bibliographic information that was readily available to the editors.

Women's Review of Books. See p. 64 below.

Women's Words. See p. 67 below.

See also these publications from **Third World Resources,** 464 19 St., Oakland, CA 94612:

Asia and Pacific: A Directory of Resources. Compiled and edited by Thomas P. Fenton and Mary J. Heffron. Maryknoll, N.Y. and London: Orbis Books and Zed Books, 1986. 160pp. $9.95, plus $1.50 shipping and handling. Illustrations and indexes.

Latin America and Caribbean: A Directory of Resources. Compiled and edited by Thomas P. Fenton and Mary J. Heffron. Maryknoll, N.Y. and London: Orbis Books and Zed Books, 1986. 160pp. $9.95, plus $1.50 shipping and handling. Illustrations and indexes.

Resource directories on Africa and on the Middle East are forthcoming from Orbis and Zed in 1987.

Third World Resource Directory: A Guide to Organizations and Publications. Edited by Thomas P. Fenton and Mary J. Heffron. Maryknoll, N.Y.: Orbis Books, 1984. 304pp. $17.95, plus $1.50 shipping and handling. Illustrations, indexes.

The books section (pp. 225-29) and the other resources section (pp. 240-43) of the chapter on women should be consulted, along with the listings of books in the other nine chapters.

Third World Resources: A Quarterly Review of Resources from and about the Third World. 4 issues/year. Newsletter. 28cm. 16pp. $25/year (organizational subscription), $25/two years (individual subscription). Inquire for overseas rates. Subscriptions are available on a calendar-year basis only.

3

Periodicals

This chapter is divided into three parts: annotated entries, supplementary list of periodicals, and sources of additional information on periodicals related to women in the Third World.

Information in the **annotated entries** is given in the following order: title; publisher; address; frequency of publication; format (magazine, newsletter, newspaper); size (height in centimeters and number of pages); subscription costs; keyword description of format; and description of content.

Quotation marks in the annotations enclose the words of the periodical's publisher, editor, or promotional materials.

Periodicals in the **supplementary list** (pp. 66–68) are grouped under these headings: Third World/International; Africa; Asia and Pacific; and Latin America and Caribbean. Information in the entries in this section is given in the following order: title; publisher; address; and type of periodical.

The **information sources** section (pp. 68–70) provides information about directories and guides that contain the names of other periodicals related to women in the Third World.

All periodical titles and related organizations in this chapter are listed in the appropriate indexes at the back of the directory. Check through the annotated entries section of the organizations chapter above for the names of additional periodicals.

ANNOTATED ENTRIES

Ahfad Journal, **University College for Women, P.O. Box 167, Omdurman, Sudan. 2 issues/year. Magazine. 24cm. 64pp. Individual and institutional subscriptions: $25/year. Feature articles, book reviews, editorials, book notices, comment and analysis.**

Established in 1984, this magazine presents "original contributions,

. . . research, literary reviews, historical or critical analyses, comments, and book reviews pertaining to the status of women in developing countries and the role of women in development as well as contributions to the family sciences, psychology and the social sciences, preschool education, and organizational management." Periodically a special issue focuses on a single topic of critical concern to women in developing countries.

Asian Women and Children, **Depth News in collaboration with the United Nations Children's Fund, Third Floor, S & L Bldg., 1500 Roxas Blvd., Manila, Philippines. 6 issues/year. Newsletter. 28cm. 8pp. Inquire for subscription rates. Feature articles, news reports, photographs, illustrations, statistical tables and figures.**

This bimonthly newsletter contains short articles on "issues concerning women and children." For example, some articles appearing in issues in 1986 pertained to nutrition in Papua New Guinea, maternity benefits for working mothers, breastfeeding in the Third World, and hospital care in Pakistan. The newsletter is attractive and easy to read. A good source for facts, it does not, however, pretend to furnish in-depth studies of any of the issues about which it reports.

Asian Women Workers Newsletter, **Committee for Asian Women, 57 Peking Rd., 5/F, Kowloon, Hongkong. 4 issues/year. Newsletter. 29.5cm. 12pp. Individual and institutional subscriptions: $4/year outside of Asia. $3/year in Asia. Feature articles, book reviews, editorials, documentation, network news, audiovisual reviews, comment and analysis, illustrations.**

Asian newspapers and other publications are the sources for the articles and news items in this newsletter. Its editors also welcome firsthand reports "on the living and working conditions of Asian workers and their struggles for equality and liberation." One issue in 1986 featured articles on "retrenchments" – plant closures, worker layoffs, and dismissals – in electronic firms in Malaysia and other parts of Southeast Asia and workers' efforts to organize. "Newsbits," a regular column, reports on, for example, women's career prospects in Korea, jobs for women in India, unions and women's rights in China, and a woman's successful suit against a Japanese trade union for discrimination.

The resources section of the newsletter is of particular interest. Books, audiovisuals, reports – all are annotated carefully and full ordering information is included.

Asian Women's Liberation, **Asian Women's Association, 211 Shibuya Co-op, 14–14 Sakuragaoka, Shibuya-ku, Tokyo 160, Japan. 1 issue/ year in English (more often in Japanese). Newsletter. 30 cm. 38pp. Individual and institutional subscriptions: $3/year. Feature articles, calendar, network news, illustrations, statistical tables.**

This newsletter's articles are of regional (Asian) interest, with international conferences, prostitution, tourism, trafficking in women, and women and military occupation among the most common topics reported.

Ch'Abuj Ri Ixoc: The Voice of the Women, **Women for Guatemala, P.O. Box 53421, Washington, DC 20009. 4 issues/year. Newsletter. 22cm. 17pp. Individual and institutional subscriptions: $10/year. Personal testimonies, action suggestions, feature articles, news reports, illustrations, charts, photographs.**

Personal testimonies of Guatemalan women form the bulk of this newsletter, which aims to show the present situation in Guatemala. Each issue focuses on a single theme: education, national independence, the family, and literacy are some examples. The women whose voices speak on the chosen topic come from a variety of backgrounds and classes.

Regular columns present synopses on human rights violations, the social, economic, and political situations, and the insurgency; the synopses are compiled from *Central America Reports,* the *Washington Post, Enfoprensa,* the *Miami Herald,* the *New York Times, Ciregua,* and other periodicals and news sources.

Change: International Reports: Women and Society, **29 Great James St., London WC1N 3ES, England. In U.S.: c/o Paula von Kleydorff, 5172 Militia Hill Rd., Plymouth Meeting, PA 19462. Occasional. Magazine. 29.5cm. 16pp. Inquire for subscription rates. Report, illustrations, statistical tables and figures.**

Change researches and publishes regular reports "on the condition and status of women all over the world." Its stated aims are "to educate and alert public opinion to the inequalities that are imposed on women through law, practice and custom . . . ; to encourage an international exchange of information . . . for overcoming obstacles to full participation by women in the development of each nation; to advance the recognition of the inalienable human rights and human dignity of women and to publicise their abuse whether by state, commercial interest or individual."

Change has an international board of advisors and correspondents. The reports are most often written by a person from the country that is the subject of the article. A 1986 issue, "Women in Pakistan: A New Era?", was written by Nighat Said Khan, a development consultant and member of the Women's Action Forum in Lahore. The publication would be useful for teachers and journalists or anyone concerned with women in a particular country.

The Church Woman, **Church Women United, 475 Riverside Dr., Rm. 812, New York, NY 10115. 4 issues/year. Magazine. 28cm. 47pp. Individual subscription: $6/year. Add $1 outside U.S. Feature articles, editorials, interviews, essays, network news, calendar, photographs, illustrations, book reviews, Bible study center-pullout.**

The Church Woman is the official publication of Church Women United, a U.S. movement of Protestant, Roman Catholic, Orthodox, and other Christian women. Although most of its articles pertain to the United States, the magazine regularly carries a section on global relationships. Profiles of women leaders in the churches from around the world and news of women's networks and international conferences bring Third World women and their views to the eight thousand subscribers.

Committee on South Asian Women Bulletin, Committee on South Asian Women, University of California, Dept. of Psychology, Rm. C-009, San Diego, CA 92093. 4 issues/year. Newsletter. 28cm. 22pp. Individual subscription: $12/year. Institutional subscription: $20/year. $8/year for students and the unemployed. Interviews, book reviews, news reports, calendar, network news, audiovisual reviews, illustrations, statistical tables, list of resources.

The *Bulletin* publishes "articles, interviews, and reviews on various aspects of the women's movement in India, Pakistan, Bangladesh, Sri Lanka, and Nepal, and on women immigrants [to the U.S.] from these countries."

The publication, a unique and useful networking tool, is sent free to women in South Asia who request it.

Of particular interest are the many notices of resources of all types available throughout the world. The newsletter regularly also reports on research being conducted by individuals and by women's groups on various topics pertinent to women in India.

Connexions, Peoples Translation Service, 4228 Telegraph Ave., Oakland, CA 94609. 4 issues/year. Magazine. 30.5cm. 32pp. Individual subscription: $10/year. Institutional subscription: $20/year. Price for single issue: $3. Inquire for other rates. Feature articles, translations, interviews, news reports, poetry, arts and literature, comment and analysis, letters to the editor, illustrations, photographs, notes, list of resources.

"One step toward building an international women's movement": this is the way the editors of *Connexions* describe their effort. Beginning in 1981, an outgrowth of a monthly newsletter of translations from the international progressive press, this international women's publication has two goals: (1) "to look beyond the borders of the United States in order to inform ourselves about the world we live in, and to connect our lives with those of women living elsewhere"; (2) "to contribute to the growth of a worldwide network connecting women working on similar projects by researching, establishing contacts and exchanging information with other women's organizations."

Recognizing the diversity of women's political, cultural, and economic situations around the world and hence their differing priorities, *Connexions* aims to contribute to their mutual understanding and appreciation and therefore to unity.

Each issue of this attractive magazine is given over to a theme. Subjects treated in 1985 and 1986 included the Nairobi conference, media, changing technology, prostitution, women and militarism, and women's movements. Contributions come from around the world: Chile, Canada, England, Pakistan, India, Nigeria, Grenada, Iran, Philippines, Namibia, Holland, West Germany, and Brazil in one issue in 1986.

Feminist Collections: A Quarterly of Women's Studies Resources,
University of Wisconsin System, Women's Studies Library, 112A Memorial Library, 728 State St., Madison, WI 53706. 4 issues/year. Newsletter. 28.5cm. 30pp. Individual subscription: $12/year. Institutional
subscription: $24/year. Subscription fee includes all publications of the
office, including *Feminist Collections* and *New Books on Women &
Feminism.* Notices of books and periodicals, book reviews, editorials,
feature articles, network news.

This quarterly publication is a very helpful source of news about the
women's movement on all levels, local to international. Much of the information is oriented toward those with a professional interest in gathering, processing, and publicizing printed materials in the women's
studies field. Thus, regular departments in the newsletter discuss issues
related to archives, feminist publishing, new reference works and periodicals, and carry news about women's studies collections in branches of
the University of Wisconsin library system.

Feminist Collections is included in the one subscription price for the
publications from the Women's Studies division of the University of
Wisconsin library named above. All are worth the attention of those
with a serious interest in women's studies resources.

Isis International Women's Journal, Isis International, Via Santa
Maria dell'Anima, 30, Rome, Italy. 4 issues/year. Magazine. 24cm.
82pp. Individual and institutional subscriptions: $25/year. Feature arti-
cles, news reports, network news, comment and analysis, illustrations,
photographs.

The English-language edition of *Isis International Bulletin* has been
published since 1976; the Spanish-language version, since 1980. In 1984
the title of the magazine was changed to *Isis International Women's
Journal* and a new way of production was instituted (two issues of the
Journal per year, with a semiannual supplement, *Women in Action*).

Isis is a quarterly publication "through which women from the different countries of the world can share ideas, information, experiences,
and models for organization and action," and for each issue since 1984 it
has worked with a particular women's group in a Third World country
who are responsible for the main content of that issue of the magazine.
This group sends one or more of its members to the Isis Rome office to
work on final production of the journal. The first such issue was produced with the Coordinating Collective of the Second Latin American
and Caribbean Feminist Meeting in Lima, Peru; the second with the
Pacific and Asian Women's Forum and Concerned Women and Media.
A 1986 issue of the journal was produced with the Committee for Asian
Women and was entitled *Industrial Women Workers in Asia.*

The *Women in Action* supplement is described as "a networking tool,
providing news and information about groups, conferences, events, and
resources—what is happening in the women's movement worldwide."

Listen Real Loud, AFSC, Nationwide Women's Program, 1501 Cherry
St., Philadelphia, PA 19102. 4 issues/year. Newsletter. 28cm. 16pp.

Individual and institutional subscriptions: $10/year. Special section = 8 pages. Regional reports, book reviews, network news, audiovisual reviews, illustrations, list of resources.

The Nationwide Women's Program of the American Friends Service Committee began publication of the *AFSC Women's Newsletter* in 1981. With the Spring 1985 issue the name was changed to *Listen Real Loud: News of Women's Liberation Worldwide,* to be published quarterly. The newsletter's aims are "to promote communication among regional, national and overseas staff, committee members and others within the AFSC orbit. The newsletter is also a vehicle for outreach to individuals and exchange with groups in the women's movement and other movements with whom we share solidarity and issue priorities."

Among the most valuable parts of the newsletter are the annotated resources section and the regular insert "Women and Global Corporations." The insert "includes reports of AFSC efforts and covers the expanding international network of individuals and groups involved in research, education, support, and direct organizing related to global industries where women are concentrated as workers or targets of consumer culture: electronics, agribusiness, textiles and the garment trades, tourism, media, and pharmaceuticals."

Manushi: A Journal about Women and Society, C1/202 Lajpat Nagar, New Delhi 110024, India. In U.S.: c/o Esther Jantzen, 5008 Erringer Place, Philadelphia, PA 19144. 6 issues/year in English; 6 issues/year in Hindi. Magazine. 27cm. 48pp. Individual subscription: $18/year. Institutional subscription: $24/year. Inquire for rates for countries other than U.S. Interviews, essays, short stories, news reports, photographs, illustrations, advertisements, classifieds, audiovisual reviews, poetry, letters.

In 1977, soon after the Emergency in India (a two-year period of political repression under the government of Indira Gandhi), a group of university women — students and teachers — "felt the need to create women's own forms of communication, to collect and disseminate [information on women's struggles in different parts of the country] . . . systematically, to begin to understand and identify the issues around which women in different parts of the country were beginning to struggle and to try to find out how we could help strengthen and spread such struggles." In a vast country like India, such networking and dissemination of information is indeed invaluable. The university group soon opened up to become a broad-based support group, "a countrywide network of support, distribution, feedback and information collection." The group decided not to accept grants from any institution or accept advertising depicting women in oppressive or stereotyped roles (a policy that they say ruled out most available ads). Their reasons for this policy were twofold: to ensure both the editorial independence of the magazine and the political and financial involvement of their supporters.

Manushi is used by thousands (it has a circulation of 15,000) of women — rural and urban — throughout India and contributes significantly to change in that country. The magazine is used in literacy programs for women, and it serves as a model for local newsletters printed in regional languages. Most articles in *Manushi* come from areas far from New Delhi. The magazine's editorial policy is "to focus on the concrete, on specific groups of women, on specific events and issues, rather than making general, sweeping statements about 'Indian women' or 'the women's movement in India.'" *Manushi*'s editors also solicit studies from women doing research in history, sociology, and anthropology, presenting such studies in simple language so that those unfamiliar with academic research can still have access to it.

This is a unique and invaluable resource for anyone who cares about women's struggles in India and in the world.

Match Newsletter, **Match International Centre, 171 Nepean, No. 401, Ottawa, Ontario K2P 0B4, Canada. 4 issues/year. Newsletter. 28cm. 8pp. Individual subscription: $10/year. Institutional subscription: $45/year. Inquire for other rates. English and French. Short articles, news reports, network news, photographs, appendixes.**

In its newsletter, Match reports on its activities and things of related interest to its member organizations throughout Canada. Contents of the quarterly regularly include reports on Match's projects around the world and news of Canadian Match chapters and of local and international conferences. The Match network supports women's projects in the Third World, fosters links between Canadian women and women in other countries and among all women interested in development, and does educational work on issues related to women and development.

Off Our Backs: A Women's News Report, **1841 Columbia Rd., NW, Rm. 212, Washington, DC 20009. 11 issues/year. Newspaper. 37.5cm. 36pp. Individual subscription: $11/year. Institutional subscription: $25/year. Free to prisoners. Feature articles, commentary and analysis, news reports, illustrations, photographs, interviews, reviews, letters, advertisements.**

Off Our Backs, published regularly since 1970, is one of the most respected of feminist news journals. Besides its regular column on international news, its feature articles are also often pertinent to Third World women's issues.

One issue from 1986, for example, carried news of a ground-breaking divorce case in India, a sexual harassment conference held in New Zealand, the Argentine legislature's discussion of a divorce bill, a report on an international conference held in Chicago on Women and the Law, and an interview with Efua Graham, a Ghanian woman, on female circumcision in Africa.

Signs: Journal of Women in Culture and Society, **University of Chicago Press, Journals Division, P.O. Box 37005, Chicago, IL 37005. 4 issues/year. Magazine. 22.5cm. 208pp. Individual subscription: $25/year. Institutional subscription: $50/year. Price for single issue: $7. Inquire for other rates. Feature articles, advertisements, book reviews, essays.**

Signs is a scholarly journal that cuts across the disciplines: "from the arts and humanities to the social sciences, from education to the natural sciences, feminist issues are central." Authors of articles represent various political perspectives—"liberal, Marxist, socialist, and radical feminist, for example."

Signs attempts to choose articles that cut across not only the disciplines but also the division between academia and women's daily lives. In 1986 selections relative to the Third World dealt with the world of Bedouin women, women workers in the Shanghai cotton mills, women in international development, and women in the Islamic Republic of Iran. The book review section is extensive and annotates many resources pertinent to Third World women.

Sister Links, Foundation for Women's Health Research and Development, Africa Centre, 38 King St., London WC2E 8JT, England, or P.O. Box A26, Cape Coast, Ghana. 4 issues/year. Magazine. 29.5cm. 18pp. Individual subscription with membership: £10 unwaged, £20 waged. Feature articles, editorials, interviews, news reports, network news, calendar, photographs, illustrations, advertisements, book reviews, letters to the editor.

This group's "principal aims are to promote good health amongst women and children through research into key areas of need, advancing action programmes aimed at meeting these needs. *Sister Links,* the foundation's development quarterly, highlights these areas of concern."

FORWARD was set up by women working in various fields of development and takes a special interest in Africa. Representative articles are on circumcision in the Sudan, forcefeeding of girls in the Sahel, feeding a family in Ghana, revolution and gains of women in the socialist revolution in Tigray (an interview), and women's education in the developing world. Issues in 1986 dealt with subjects such as traditional healing versus Western medicines and ill health and the position of women in society.

Sister Links began publication in 1985 and "contains material from women themselves giving *their* views on all subjects which form our reality."

The Tribune: Women and Development Quarterly, International Women's Tribune Centre, 777 UN Plaza, New York, NY 10017. 4 issues/ year. Magazine. 27cm. 32pp. English, Spanish, and French. Individual and institutional subscriptions: $8/year. $10/year in Europe, Australia, and New Zealand. Free to persons in the Third World. Short reports, project news, action suggestions, book notices, audiovisual reviews, list of resources.

The Tribune is an information service and the official organ of the International Women's Tribune Centre network. The newsletter is one of the ways by which the IWTC "collects and disseminates information of a practical nature to and about women in developmental activities." One series of newsletters explored the topic "Women and Water"; another, "Technology and Small Business: Women's Perspectives."

The newsletter describes itself as a unique combination of text and graphics. Each issue identifies specific goals for the international women's movement and describes the obstacles to those goals. Articles present examples from around the world of strategies and projects that relate to these goals and obstacles, offers suggestions for action, and gives detailed listings of resources of all types. News from the United Nations pertinent to women is included in some issues.

WIN News, **Women's International Network, 187 Grant St., Lexington, MA 02173. 4 issues/year. Magazine. 28cm. 84pp. Individual subscription: $20/year. Institutional subscription: $30/year. $3 postage outside the United States. Listings of job openings, editorials, news reports, calendar, columnists, network news, book notices, list of resources.**

WIN News, published regularly since 1975, was one of the first magazines dedicated to news and networking on women's issues. It describes itself as "a worldwide, open communication system run by, for, and about women of all backgrounds, beliefs, nationalities, and age groups. [It] serves the general public, institutions, and organizations by transmitting internationally information about women and women's groups."

About half of each issue is devoted to news items and resources related to these and similar topics: women and the UN, women and health, female circumcision/genital mutilation, women and development, women and environment, women and violence, women and media, and women and international affairs: clearinghouse (international career opportunities for women).

Reports from around the world comprise the other half of each issue. Each issue then concludes with a section on international information. The pages given over to each heading are packed with detailed information on conferences, meetings, trips, organizations, projects, and printed and audiovisual resources. The information furnished on every item is complete enough to satisfy anybody wishing to attend a conference, buy a book, rent a film, or join an organization.

Wiser Links, **173 Archway Rd., London N16 5AB, England. 6 issues/year. Newsletter. 29.5cm. 16pp. Individual and institutional subscriptions: £6/year. Inquire for other rates. Feature articles, book reviews, news reports, calendar, letters to the editor, illustrations, notes, list of resources.**

Wiser Links is a modest newsletter published by a group that began networking in June 1983. The group's aim is to set up "information and exchange links with women worldwide" and to "promote dialogue and encourage direct links between women's organizations with similar concerns in Western and Third World countries."

Women at Work, **International Labour Office, CH–1211, Geneva 22, Switzerland. 2 issues/year. Magazine. Individual and institutional subscriptions: $11.50/year. Published in French and English. Reports on trends, documentation, news reports, statistical tables.**

This news bulletin of the ILO reports on the "economic and social contribution of women to society," on recent trends in these areas, and on international comparative information on issues pertinent to women and work: promotion of equality, work and family, job options and training, maternity protection, working conditions, participation in trade unions and management, and developments in UN bodies and agencies. The bulletin also contains official documents and bibliographical listings. A cumulative index is available.

Woman Speak!, **Women and Development Unit (WAND), University of the West Indies, Extra-Mural Dept., Pinelands, St. Michael, Barbados. 4 issues/year. Newsletter. 28cm. 22pp. Individual and institutional subscriptions: $8/year. Regional calendar, book reviews, editorials, feature articles, news reports, poetry, letters to the editor, illustrations, statistical tables, list of resources.**

This is a quarterly newsletter about Caribbean women; it has published since 1979. It deals with such issues as women in food marketing, women and disability, women and credit, women and the law, women and work, women and health, women and agriculture, and young women. It reviews news of local or regional organizations such as the Jamaica Bureau of Women's Affairs. Its December 1985 issue was a double issue on the Nairobi conference.

Womenews, **Women Studies and Research Center, c/o GABRIELA, Santos Bldg., 2nd fl., Gen. Malvar Ext., Davao City, Philippines. 4 issues/year. Newsletter. 30cm. 12pp. Individual and institutional subscriptions: $12/year. Feature articles, interviews, news reports, network news, poetry, letters to the editor, illustrations, photographs.**

Until the overthrow of the Marcos regime in early 1986 *Womenews* reported extensively on women detainees in the Philippines. Under the new government articles will deal with research on plantation workers (a large number of whom are women), and the GABRIELA (General Assembly Binding Women for Reforms, Integrity, Equality, Leadership and Action, founded in 1984, 59 organizations affiliated as of March 1985) activities.

Women's News Digest, **Association for Advancement of Feminism, 17–23 Thomson Rd., Rm. 1202, Wanchai, Hongkong. 6 issues/year. Newsletter. 29.5cm. 12pp. Individual and institutional subscriptions: $5/year. News reports, illustrations.**

This publication, launched in 1986, reprints articles from the Hongkong English-language newspapers. Its stated purposes are "to record and make known the situation of women in Hongkong and in China . . . [and to] highlight the problems and issues faced by women in this part of the world — ones they share with sisters in other Asian countries and in other continents."

The articles are arranged by topic: family, education, abortion, health, politics. A *Chinese Women's News Digest* is also available; it reprints articles from ten Hongkong Chinese-language newspapers.

Women's Review of Books, **Wellesley College Center for Research on Women, 828 Washington St., Wellesley, MA 02181. 12 issues/year. Newspaper. 42cm. 20pp. Individual subscription: $14/year. Institutional** subscription: $25/year. Book reviews and notices, advertisements, audiovisual reviews, poetry, arts and literature, letters to the editor, photographs.

This review is an invaluable tool for anyone looking for resources on women. The reviews, booklists, and ads all contain information on books and audiovisual materials.

The review's policy is "feminist but not restricted to any one conception of feminism. . . . We seek to represent the widest possible range of feminist perspectives both in the books reviewed and in the content of the reviews. We believe that no one of us, alone or in a group, can speak for feminism, or women, as such; all of our thinking and writing takes place in a specific political, social, ethnic and sexual context, and a responsible review periodical should reflect and further that diversity."

Women's Studies International Forum, Pergamon Press, Maxwell House, Fairview Park, Elmsford, NY 10523. 6 issues/year. Magazine. 24.5cm. 160pp. Individual subscription: $40/year. Institutional subscription: $95/year. Abstracts, advertisements, editorials, feature articles, documentation, network news, statistical tables.

Women's Studies International Forum is a "multidisciplinary journal for the rapid publication of research communications and review articles in women's studies" that began publication in 1978. The journal encourages international exchange and does not limit the source of its articles to academia. The special issue (vol. 8, no. 4, 1985) containing selections from the Second International Interdisciplinary Congress on Women included articles on women and poverty in Bangladesh, Kenyan women, and strategies for action.

A newsletter, *Feminist Forum,* comes with a subscription to *Women's Studies.* It contains abstracts from the panels of recent conferences, calls for papers for future conferences, announcements of new publications and organizations, and reports on, for example, "The Women's Movement: A Latin American Perspective" (vol. 8, no. 4, 1985).

Women's World, Isis-WICCE, P.O. Box 2471, 1211 Geneva, Switzerland. 4 issues/year. Magazine. 42cm. 12pp. Individual subscription: $10/year. Institutional subscription: $20/year. Feature articles, advertisements, action suggestions, book reviews, editorials, news reports, calendar, network news, poetry, photographs.

Women's World is really three publications: *Newsletter, Report,* and *Dossier.* Each reflects a particular facet of Isis-WICCE's focus as an organization on the links between the situation of women in developing and industrial countries from a feminist perspective. The organization chooses one theme each year as its primary emphasis for all its programs and publications. In 1984, the focus was women and communication; in 1985, women and health; in 1986, women and technology.

The *Newsletter* presents "news of events, groups and publications about women worldwide and tells about the latest developments in the Exchange Programme" (Women's International Cross Cultural Exchange). A full page or more is devoted to reporting on resources.

The *Dossier* is an anthology of articles, papers, and resources on the current focus of Isis–WICCE's activities. The *Dossier* on women and health, for example, was "prepared as a background document for the Third Isis–WICCE Exchange Programme." Each of the three chapters focused on one of the following: women's experiences (of the medical system, menstruation, menopause, contraception, sexuality, and sexually transmitted diseases); the forces damaging the health of all human beings (poverty, hunger, drugs, chemical and environmental pollution, and stress); and action (women's self-help movement, organizing around issues, lobbying). Each chapter contained a list of resources.

The *Report* presents the experiences of the participants in the organization's exchange program.

In all, the publications present an impressive and attractive collection of documentation, resources, opinions, and experiences from women all over the world.

SUPPLEMENTARY LIST OF PERIODICALS

THIRD WORLD/INTERNATIONAL

Broadsheet, P.O. Box 5799, Wellesley St., Auckland, New Zealand. Newsletter.

CCSA SACC, 874 rue Sherbrooke E., Montreal, Quebec H2L 1K9, Canada. Newsletter.

Communiqu'elle, Les Éditions Communiqu'elle, 3585 St-Urbain, Montreal, Quebec H2X 2N6, Canada.

International Journal of Women, Eden Press Women, 245 Victoria Ave., Suite 12, Montreal, Quebec H3Z 2M6, Canada.

Journal of Women and Religion, Center for Women and Religion of the Graduate Theological Union, 2465 LeConte Ave., Berkeley, CA 94709.

The Longest Revolution, Center for Women's Studies and Services, P.O. Box 350, San Diego, CA 92101.

Media Report to Women, Women's Institute for Freedom of the Press, 3306 Ross Pl., NW, Washington, DC 20008.

MS Magazine, 119 W. 40 St., New York, NY 10018. Magazine.

La Mujer Feminista, Apartado de Correos 311, Madrid, Spain.

Out!, Multi-National Women's Liberation Group, 69 Mauromichali, Athens, Greece. Newsletter.

Outwrite, Oxford House, Derbyshire St., London E2, England.

Plexus, 545 Athol Ave., Oakland, CA 94606. Newspaper.

Spare Rib: A Women's Liberation Magazine, 27 Clerkenwell Close, London EC1, England. tabloid newspaper.

Transnational Perspectives, Case Postal 161, 1211 Geneva 16, Switzerland.

Woman of Power: A Magazine of Feminism, Spirituality, and Politics, P.O. Box 827, Cambridge, MA 02238. Magazine.

Women: A Journal of Liberation, 3028 Greenmount Ave., Baltimore, MD 21218. Magazine.

Women and Environments, Centre for Urban and Community Studies, 455 Spadina Ave., Toronto, Ontario M5S 2G8, Canada.

Women of the Whole World: Journal of the Women's International Democratic Federation, Unter den Linden 13, 1018 Berlin, German Democratic Republic. Magazine.

Women's Words, Kathy McLaughlin, 8 Fort Point St., #12, East Norwalk, CT 06855. Newsletter.

AFRICA

Federation of African Media Features Service, Federation of African Media Women, P.O. Box 50795, Nairobi, Kenya.

Ideal Woman, P.O. Box 57357, House #F, 800/1, Cantonments Rd., Accra North, Ghana. Magazine.

Voice of Women, African National Congress, 801 Second Ave., Suite 405, New York, NY 10017. Newsletter.

ASIA AND PACIFIC

The Awakening, 12F-1, 431 Kuang-fu South Rd., Taipei, Taiwan.

AWRAN Newsletter, Asian Women's Research and Action Network, P.O. Box 208, Davao City, Philippines. Newsletter.

Bulletin of the CWDS, Center for Women's Development Studies, B-43, Panchsheel Enclave, New Delhi 110017, India. Newsletter.

Depthnews Women, P.O. Box 1843, Manila, Philippines. Newsletter.

Friends of Women, 2/3 Soi Wang-Lang, Arunamarin Rd., Bangkok 10700, Thailand.

Korean Women Today, Korean Women, C.P.O. Box 2267, Seoul, Korea.

Ofis Blong Ol Meri Newsletter, Ofis Blong Ol Meri, P.O. Box 1327, Lae, Papua New Guinea. Newsletter.

Samya Shakti: A Journal of Women, Center for Women, B-43, Panch-sheel Enclave, New Delhi 110017, India.

Voice of Women: Sri Lanka Journal for Women, 18/9 Chitra Lane, Colombo 5, Sri Lanka. Newsletter.

WAF, Women's Action Forum, P.O. Box 3287, Gulberg, Lahore, Pakistan. Magazine.

Women of China, 50 Deng Shi Kou, Beijing, China. Magazine.

Women's Link, Christian Conference of Asia, Women's Desk, 480, Lorong 2, Toa Payoh, Singapore 1231, Singapore. Newsletter.

LATIN AMERICA AND CARIBBEAN

La Cacerola, GRECMU, Juan Paulier 1174, Montevideo, Uruguay.

fem, Av. Mexico No. 76-1, Col. Progreso Tizapan, Mexico 20, DF, Mexico.

María, Liberación del Pueblo, Apdo. 158-B, Ave. Morelos 714, Cuernavaca, Morelos, Mexico.

Mujer and *Fempress,* Unidad de Comunicación Alternativa de la Mujer, Casilla 16-637, Correo 9, Santiago, Chile.

Mujer CEFEMINA, Apdo. 949, San José, Costa Rica.

Mujer/ILET, Latin American Women, Casilla 16-637, Correo 9, Santiago, Chile.

Mulherio, Fundação Carlos Chagas, Caixa Postal 11352, 05499 São Paulo, Brazil.

Sistren, Sistren Theatre Collective, 20 Kensington Crescent, Kingston 5, Jamaica. Newsletter.

La Tortuga, Huancavelica 470, Oficina 408, Lima, Peru.

Ventana, Apartado 925, Centro Colon, San José, Costa Rica.

INFORMATION SOURCES

The following publications are noteworthy for the lists and descriptive information they provide on periodicals related to women in the Third World:

The Annotated Guide to Women's Periodicals in the U.S. Compiled and edited by Terry Mehlman, 5173 Turner Rd., Richmond, IN 47374. Biannual.

Feminist Periodicals: A Current Listing of Contents. Published by Susan Searing, Women's Studies Librarian-at-Large, University of Wisconsin System, 112A Memorial Library, 728 State St., Madison, WI 53706. 4 issues/year. 28cm. 52pp. Individuals and women's programs: $12/year. Institutional subscription: $24/year. Subscription fee includes all publications of the office, including *Feminist Collections: A Quarterly of Women's Studies Resources, New Books on Women & Feminism,* and bibliographies, directories, and occasional publications.

Feminist Periodicals is intended to "serve several purposes: to keep the reader abreast of current topics in feminist literature; to increase readers' familiarity with a wide spectrum of feminist periodicals; and to provide the requisite bibliographic information should a reader wish to subscribe to a journal or to obtain a particular article at her library or through interlibrary loan."

Tables of contents from current issues of more than one hundred major feminist journals are reproduced in each issue of *Feminist Periodicals;* they are preceded by a comprehensive annotated listing of all journals received at the Office of the Women's Studies Librarian-at-Large.

The editors strive to include "all English-language feminist periodicals with a substantial national or regional readership, with an emphasis on scholarly journals and small press offerings. [*Feminist Periodicals* does] not include publications which, though feminist in philosophy, do not focus solely on women's issues. Nor, with the exception of *Ms.,* do we include newsstand magazines."

Guide to Women's Publishing. Edited by Polly Joan and Andrea Chesman. Paradise, Calif.: Dustbooks, 1978.

Index/Directory of Women's Media. Washington, D.C.: Women's Institute for Freedom of the Press, annual.

This directory lists hundreds of women's organizations and individuals relevant to media and the women's movement. Names and addresses are given for periodicals, women's presses, publishers, news services, film groups, theater, bookstores, and distributors.

Women's Periodicals and Newspapers from the Eighteenth Century to 1981. Edited by James P. Danky. Compiled by Maureen E. Hady, Barry Christopher Noonan, and Neil E. Strache. Boston: G. K. Hall, 1982. 376pp.

This is a guide to the contents and locations of nearly 1,500 periodicals and newspaper titles that are related to women that were received in the Library of the State Historical Society of Wisconsin before July 1981, the libraries of the University of Wisconsin–Madison, and other public, academic, and special libraries in the greater Madison area. Entries are annotated and indexed by geographical area, editors, publishers, subjects, languages, subtitles, and chronology.

Periodicals such as *Connexions* and *Isis International Women's Journal* regularly carry lists of magazines, newsletters, and newspapers that focus on women. The International Women's Tribune Centre is preparing an updated and expanded edition of a publication it first issued in September 1984 with lists of periodicals around the world that have provided information on activities related to the Decade for Women.

In addition there are standard library resources, such as *The IMS Ayer Directory of Publications* and *Ulrich's International Periodicals Directory.*

See also these publications from **Third World Resources,** 464 19 St., Oakland, CA 94612:

Asia and Pacific: A Directory of Resources. Compiled and edited by Thomas P. Fenton and Mary J. Heffron. Maryknoll, N.Y., and London: Orbis Books and Zed Press, 1986. 160pp. $9.95, plus $1.50 shipping and handling. Illustrations and indexes.

Latin America and Caribbean: A Directory of Resources. Compiled and edited by Thomas P. Fenton and Mary J. Heffron. Maryknoll, N.Y., and London: Orbis Books and Zed Books, 1986. 160pp. $9.95, plus $1.50 shipping and handling. Illustrations and indexes.

Resource directories on Africa and on the Middle East are forthcoming from Orbis and Zed in 1987.

Third World Resource Directory: A Guide to Organizations and Publications. Edited by Thomas P. Fenton and Mary J. Heffron. Maryknoll, N.Y.: Orbis Books, 1984. 304pp. $17.95, plus $1.50 shipping and handling. Illustrations, indexes.

The periodicals section (pp. 229–30) of the chapter on women should be consulted, along with the listings of periodicals in the other nine chapters.

Third World Resources: A Quarterly Review of Resources from and about the Third World. 4 issues/year. Newsletter. 28cm. 16pp. $25/year (organizational subscription), $25/two years (individual subscription). Inquire for overseas rates. Subscriptions are available on a calendar-year basis only.

4

Pamphlets and Articles

The aim of this chapter is to present printed resource materials that are self-contained (usually an entire issue of a magazine on one topic), brief, inexpensive, and easily available, often at bulk rates.

The dividing line between a book and a pamphlet (or booklet) is a thin one at times. The rule of thumb used to distinguish between the two was: bound, printed materials that numbered less than one hundred pages, were priced at less than $5, or were one volume of a serial publication are listed in the pamphlets and articles chapter. Admittedly this dividing line is arbitrary, and it is hoped that no author will be offended that her/his work is classed as a "pamphlet." Resources in this chapter are no less important because they are concise.

This chapter is divided into three parts: annotated entries, supplementary list of pamphlets and articles, and sources of additional information on pamphlets and articles.

Information in the **annotated entries** is given in the following order: author(s) or editor(s); title; publisher; periodical name; publication data (volume, number, date); number of pages; price; keyword description of format; and description of content.

Pamphlets and articles in the **supplementary list** (pp. 97–101) are grouped under these headings: Third World; Africa; Asia and Pacific; Latin America and Caribbean; and Middle East. Information in the entries in this section is given in the following order: author(s) or editor(s); title; publisher; name of periodical; publication data; number of pages; and price.

The **information sources** section (pp. 101–102) provides information about directories and guides that contain the names of other articles and pamphlets related to women in the Third World.

The titles of all the entries in this chapter are integrated into the titles index at the back of the directory. See the organizations index for addresses of publishers or distributors that appear in this chapter. (Note that whenever the names of the publisher and the periodical are identical, the names will appear in both the titles and organizations indexes.)

ANNOTATED ENTRIES

Agarwhal, Bina, and Kamla Bhasin, eds. *Women and Media: Analysis, Alternatives, and Action.* **Isis International and Pacific and Asian Women's Forum.** *Isis International Women's Journal,* **Dec. 1984. 132pp. $4. Articles, poetry, illustrations, photographs, bibliography, list of resources.**

Women and Media describes and analyses "the many commonalities that exist in the sexist distortions of media's portrayal of women, across the non-socialist countries — developed and developing."

At the same time the booklet focuses attention on certain aspects of media that have significant implications for the Third World. The latter include: (1) "anti-women biases" in the so-called development communications media used by both government and private voluntary organizations to promote economic development programs, and (2) the tendency to think of media strictly as technological, ignoring the fact that people have traditionally been the means of communication in Third World countries and that the content of much of this "people's communication" is drawn from culturally rooted (and often biased) religious and mythical philosophies.

The second half of *Women and Media* describes attempts made by various women's groups in India and elsewhere both to "protest against existing negative portrayals and to create alternatives." This very issue of the *Women's Journal,* the editors conclude, may be seen as "an alternative, a new method of functioning." Edited and produced entirely in India, *Women and Media* is actually a joint production of three organizations: Isis International (Rome and Santiago), the Pacific and Asian Women's Forum, and Kali for Women, a feminist press.

Aguilar, Mila D. *A Comrade Is as Precious as a Rice Seedling.* **Kitchen Table: Women of Color Press. 1984. 38pp. $4.50. Poetry, illustrations.**

"The poetry of Mila Aguilar," writes Audre Lorde in the foreword to this slim volume, "does what poetry is supposed to do, evoke the experiences out of which the poems come so tellingly that there is no choice but to feel the weight of that commitment from which the words draw their power."

Mila Aguilar's commitment was put to the test during a two-year imprisonment for "subversion and conspiracy to commit rebellion" against the dictatorship of Ferdinand Marcos. Now that she has won her freedom (under the government of Cory Aquino) it can be stated openly and without fear of harmful repression against her that this young educator and poet is indeed a rebel and a subversive. Her poems give eloquent testimony to that fact.

She despises the "underhandedness of the bourgeoisie." She ridicules the "mothers" who strut around on polished parquet floors boasting about the successes of their children. And she damns "the US-Marcos dictatorship" that created "rice queues longer than any vaunted seventh longest bridge in the world" and that siphoned off the riches of the Philippines "to America and Japan."

Marcos was correct. It was just such determined passion that posed the greatest threat to his regime. Marcos has fled. A battle has been won. The day now belongs to Mila Aguilar and the legions of her comrades who—like rice seedlings—"will give birth to many more who will fill the hunger of generations of peasants for food, and land, and right."

Alexandre, Laurien. *Impressions of Forum '85.* **Immaculate Heart College Center.** *Global Pages,* **3, no. 4 (Aug./Sept. 1985). 16pp. Free. Feature articles, illustrations, tables, photographs, list of resources.**

Reports abound on the conference in Nairobi, Kenya, that closed the United Nations Decade of Women in 1985. This one, by the editor of *Global Pages,* is concise, well-written, and attractively presented.

A four-page introduction records Alexandre's "Impressions of Forum '85." History's largest gathering of and for women, she writes, deepened her "personal understanding of what it means to be born female" and made concrete her "abstract concepts about women's potential in the world economic, political, and social order."

Alexandre next discusses the conference's attempts to reconceptualize development theory and planning "from an inherently feminist perspective, one that takes into account the role of women and an integrated approach to overall human needs."

The centerfold presents a summary of information on women and the family, agriculture, industrialization, health, education, and politics.

Beyond Stereotypes: Asian Women in Development. **Southeast Asia Resource Center.** *Southeast Asia Chronicle* **96 (Jan. 1985). 34pp. $2.50. Photographs, tables, notes, resource guide, complete backlist of the** *Southeast Asia Chronicle* **(July 1971 through January 1985, the final issue). Available from the Asia Resource Center (Washington, D.C.) and the Philippine Resource Center (Berkeley, Calif.).**

"Our treatment of Asian women caught in the process called development," say the editors of this issue of the *Chronicle,* "is not a litany of distress for victims. Certainly, articles in this issue describe exploitation and hardship, but they also highlight the resourcefulness and personal dignity with which women throughout Asia are responding to their circumstances."

Contents: "Industrialization and Prostitution in Southeast Asia" by Aihwa Ong; "In Pursuit of an Illusion: Thai Women in Europe" and "Three Women" by Siriporn Skrobanek; "Friends of Women" by Chris Jenkins; "Making a Living: South Korean Women in Commerce" by Pilwhat Chang-Michell; "Offering Support: Maternity Leave and Childcare" by Vu Thi Chin; and "From Birth Control to Population Control" by Lynn Duggan.

Bond-Stewart, Kathy, with Leocardia Chimbaudi Mudimu, eds. Photographs by Biddy Partridge. *Young Women in the Liberation Struggle: Stories and Poems from Zimbabwe.* Zimbabwe Publishing House. 1984. 67pp. $3. Photographs.

This is one of the Women of Africa Series published by Zimbabwe Publishing House in Harare. The stories and poems in this collection were chosen from magazines produced during the editors' English courses taught to 250 women over a period of eighteen months. The women chose the themes: survival, courage, the third struggle, improvements, progress.

These young women write in simple but striking terms of the liberation of Zimbabwe, their country. Their stories and poems tell of their childhoods, their decisions to become fighters, their experiences of war, death, friendship, victory, and their continuing effort to make a strong and just society. They write in the introduction to the book: "We as former freedom fighters mustn't leave the struggle incomplete . . . We would like to show the world that we can produce something magnificent."

Bryceson, Deborah Fahy. *Women and Technology in Developing Countries: Technological Change and Women's Capabilities.* UN International Research and Training Institute for the Advancement of Women (INSTRAW). *Research Study,* no. 1–C, May 1985. 44pp. References, statistical tables, bibliography.

The argument put forward in this paper is that "technological change leads to changes in the content and inter-relationship [among] the household, market and state, and in turn the bargaining positions, responsibilities and capabilities of women and men in these social institutions change." Not surprisingly these changes have resulted in increased opportunities for men in the spheres of state and market, while women have become increasingly estranged "from many developments in production, exploration, and destruction" outside the home.

The author, of St. Anthony's College, Oxford, believes that it is a mistake to think that "these three institutions [household, market, and state] can just be left to drift with technological change and by chance bring about an improvement in women's bargaining positions and increase the scope for women's realization of their human capabilities."

There is "an urgent need," she concludes, "for communities of women and men in both rural and urban areas to democratically exchange ideas and work towards defining a new, more equitable division of social responsibilities between the sexes in conjunction with decisions on the content and form of technical change." "Desired types of technological change should be collectively discussed and acted upon at the community level," Bryceson insists.

Bryceson contributes her own analysis and policy recommendations to the discussion she calls for, along with an eight-page bibliography on these issues.

Bunch, Charlotte. *Bringing the Global Home: Feminism in the '80s.* **Antelope Publications. 1985. 44pp. $3.50. List of resources.**

This essay by a leading figure in the international women's movement considers the ways in which women can "learn from each other and develop a global perspective within each of our [regional] movements." Global feminism, Bunch states, "means expansion of our understandings of feminism and changes in our work, as we respond to the ideas and challenges of women coming from different perspectives. It means discovering what other perspectives and movements mean to our own local setting."

The author discusses the need to make connections among issues such as the economic and sexual exploitation of women and militarism and racism. She encourages her readers to learn from diversity, to examine critically "cultural" practices that oppress women, and to think globally and act locally.

Antelope Publications is a feminist publishing house that is committed to reviving "the art of political pamphleteering by printing edited versions of contemporary speeches, workshops, and lectures which comment on and analyze the political and social lives of women from a feminist perspective." Two other essays by Charlotte Bunch are available from Antelope: *Facing Down the Right* (24pp. $2) and *Going Public with Our Vision* (28pp. $3).

Buvinić, Mayra. *Projects for Women in the Third World: Explaining Their Misbehavior.* **International Center for Research on Women. April 1984. 30pp. $5. Diagram, references, bibliography.**

This ICRW study tries to explain how and why most income-generation projects for women in the Third World "misbehave," that is, degenerate into welfare projects when they were designed to expand employment and economic opportunities for poor women. The author concludes that the motives of the project planners are not to blame, but that there are factors "in the environment and characteristics of projects" that explain this failure.

On the environmental level, Buvinić says, "welfare approaches prevail because welfare-oriented action is perceived to have low anticipated costs." As to the projects' characteristics, there are, according to the author, numerous obstacles to successful implementation of projects for women. Among these are: (1) "a preference for stereotypical female tasks and the misjudgment that these tasks are simple and transferable to poor women," (2) "the use of volunteer staff to implement projects," and (3) "participatory activities that require low-income women to volunteer their time and labor."

The paper closes with suggestions for ways to reverse the welfare orientation of projects for Third World women. It proposes roles for women-only agencies in research, policy-making, and advocacy, but argues that the implementation of projects should be done by integrated agencies.

Research for this study was funded in part by the U.S. Agency for International Development.

Chaney, Elsa M. *Scenarios of Hunger in the Caribbean.* **Women in International Development, Michigan State University.** *Working Papers on Women in International Development,* **no. 18, 1983. 31pp. $3. References, bibliography.**

Concentrating particularly on the Jamaican situation, this paper searches for the root causes of hunger and malnutrition in the English-speaking Caribbean in these four areas: (1) high levels of "outmigration" from the rural areas to the cities, as well as "foreign" migration by thousands of West Indians to England, Canada, and the United States; (2) declining productivity in the small farm sector that raises the domestic foods that poor people eat; (3) the "feminization of farming," with women taking on more and more responsibility for both food and cash crops without receiving the supports they need; and (4) "overdependency on food purchased from abroad and scarcity of foreign exchange to buy it."

Chaney, an associate of the Equity Policy Center (Washington, D.C.), cites these statistics to illustrate the precarious situation of the poor in Jamaica: "The most important items in the diet of the Jamaican poor, after sugar, are flour and rice—95 percent of which are imported. Lower-income groups—calculated at about 70 percent of the population, who spend 80 percent of their income on food—depend upon sugar, flour and rice as their most important sources of energy, and on flour, rice and bread as their principal sources of protein."

Chaney's solutions to the problems she describes and analyzes are to strengthen national nutrition policy (linking food consumption and nutritional issues to agricultural policies) and to increase the emphasis on smallholder agriculture (without doing away with cash crops in the process).

Changing Technology. **Peoples Translation Service.** *Connexions,* **no. 15, Winter 1985. 32pp. $3. Translated feature articles, advertisements, illustrations, photographs, references, list of resources.**

"Clearly," write the editors of this issue of *Connexions,* "despite the benign image of dedicated researchers pushing forward the frontiers of knowledge, scientists, who are predominantly white and male, do bring their own ideologies to bear in choosing and pursuing research topics. To an even greater degree, those who fund and thereby control the directions of science are also white and male." "Sexism and racism," the editors conclude, "are inherent in this military/industrial/technological science."

Changing Technology explores questions that confront women today: how to make informed choices regarding technology, how to direct and integrate technology into their daily lives, and how to use their limited resources to acquire appropriate technologies. "Furthermore," say the editors, "women must be actively involved in the politics of development in order to ensure that their nation's planning and importation of technology responds to their needs and contributes to their independence, not dependence."

Articles are translated or reproduced from publications in India, Australia, Uruguay, Kenya, Sri Lanka, China, Mexico, and numerous other nations.

Chinchilla, Norma S. *Women in Revolutionary Movements: The Case of Nicaragua.* Women in International Development, Michigan State University. *Working Papers on Women in International Development,* no. 27, 1983. 19pp. $2.50. References.

The participation of women in Central American revolutionary movements has surpassed, in quantity and quality, all previous examples in the history of the Western hemisphere and, perhaps, the world, according to Dr. Chinchilla. Looking particularly at Nicaragua the author searches for the factors that explain this phenomenon. The ones she identifies as being "the most important elements" for a theory of women's participation in revolutionary movements in general or in Central America particularly are: (1) the international context in which the revolutions are taking place (the impact of the international women's movement and the experience of women in revolutionary movements in other Third World countries); (2) contradictions in the internal social structure of Central American societies that affect women directly (migration, male unemployment, female-headed families, influx of women into higher education, etc.); (3) conditions for women within the revolutionary movement and in revolutionary organizations (leadership, revolutionary relations between men and women, revolutionary ethics, etc.); and (4) the general line and strategy of the revolutionary movement, particularly the line of "prolonged people's war."

The author, a professor at California State University (Long Beach), examines each of these factors and concludes that the Central American revolutions "represent some of the most hopeful advances yet" in forging links between Marxism as a method and strategy of revolutionary transformation.

Cho, Uhn, and Hagen Koo. *Capital Accumulation, Women's Work, and Informal Economies in Korea.* Women In International Development, Michigan State University. *Working Papers on Women in International Development,* no. 21, 1983. 18pp. $2.50. Notes, statistical tables.

The authors of this study correct two misperceptions about women's roles in development. First, they describe the ways in which women have been, and are, always integrated into the economic processes of society. They do not need to be "integrated" into development, as many development theorists suggest. Second, they explain how most developmentalists assume that only those activities of women that are included in the calculation of the Gross National Product (GNP) contribute to national development.

Having disposed of these misperceptions the two professors (Cho at Dong-Guk University and Koo at the University of Hawaii) turn to a detailed study of the relationship between economic development and women's work in one rapidly industrializing country, South Korea. The question they address is how women's economic activities have changed in relation to the pattern of economic growth in South Korea in the past two decades.

Analysis of labor statistics and the results of a sample survey reveal these changes: (1) the absorption of female workers into the industrial sector has been faster than that of male workers; (2) rural women have had to assume a larger role in agricultural work due to the increasing shortage of labor in rural areas; and (3) active involvement of married women in various forms of informal earning activities has grown considerably.

Committee for Asian Women. *Tales of the Filipino Working Women.* **Christian Conference of Asia–Urban Rural Mission. June 1984. 68pp. $2.50. Map, illustrations.**

From all over the rural Philippines young women come to Manila, the "Dream City," in hopes of escaping a life of poverty and deprivation, of helping younger children in the family to get an education, of getting an education themselves. Most begin as housemaids, salespersons, or workers in small factories. The women whose lives are described in this booklet eventually found themselves working for foreign firms in the garment, textile, or electronics industries.

Their very personal stories tell of poor working conditions, low wages, unrealistic quotas and work hours, health problems, lack of job security, and exposure to toxics. Their stories, told in the first person in simple, straightforward style, are also of militancy, organization, union activities, and always of struggle.

Flora, Cornelia Butler. *Socialist Feminism in Latin America.* **Women in International Development, Michigan State University.** *Working Papers on Women in International Development,* **no. 14, 1982. 27pp. $2.75.**

The author of this article begins by pointing out the many "stances" or faces of the women's movement throughout the world that are not important "in women's politics in most of Latin America." She maintains that "socialist feminism" is one of the "leading forces of the Latin American women's movement" and she describes it as "concerned with many of the same sources of oppression as leftist groups and the progressive church in Latin America." It "tries to unite the problems of gender oppression with those of class oppression."

The study is based on several years' work with women's groups in eight countries of Latin America when the author was a member of the Ford Foundation staff and later a consultant from the United States helping develop Foundation women's programs. The author examines the origins of socialist feminism, the differences among feminist groups in the many Latin American countries, and international linkages. She presents movements in Brazil, Peru, the Dominican Republic, and Chile as brief case studies.

Forum '85. Nairobi, Kenya. **Peoples Translation Service.** *Connexions,* **no. 17-18, Summer/Fall 1985. 64pp. $5. Feature articles, illustrations, photographs, references, list of resources.**

The conference that officially brought the United Nations Decade for Women to a close is the focus of this issue of *Connexions.* Nairobi was the site for Forum '85, a gathering of representatives from Non-Governmental Organizations (NGO), as well as for the official UN conference.

Forum '85 covers all aspects of the NGO conference — from the nuts-and-bolts of housing in Kenya's capital city to transcriptions from the conference workshops. A lengthy introduction and an interview with a leading Mexican feminist, Claudia Hinojosa, set the Nairobi meeting into its historical context, following the Mexico City meeting that opened the Decade for Women and the midpoint conference in Copenhagen.

Fittingly, *Forum '85* devotes a good deal of its coverage to the situation of women in Kenya itself. Other articles cover subjects such as transnational corporations, peace, law, technology, and female circumcision.

As is their custom the *Connexions* staff provides recommended readings at the conclusion of many of the articles. This special double issue concludes with a jam-packed, two-page listing of international periodicals by, for, and about women.

Fuentes, Annette, and Barbara Ehrenreich. *Women in the Global Factory.* **South End Press. 1983. 64pp. $4.75. Photographs, illustrations, statistical tables, notes, bibliography, list of resources.**

Young Third World women are today's "factory girls," a "giant reserve army of labor at the disposal of globetrotting multinationals." This booklet examines their exploitative situation, their strategic importance, and their increasing militancy.

Two chapters of the booklet are given over to a study of women workers in two areas of the Third World: East Asia and Mexico. The material is clearly and attractively presented. No one who reads it will look unthinkingly at a "Made in Korea" label again.

Gallin, Rita S. *Rural Industrialization and Chinese Women: A Case Study from Taiwan.* **Women in International Development, Michigan State University.** *Working Papers on Women in International Development,* **no. 47, 1984. 21pp. $2.75. Notes, statistical tables, references.**

The purpose of this paper is to examine how Taiwan's export-oriented industrialization is built on the backs of the women of Taiwan. Basing her conclusions on field research carried out intermittently from 1957 through 1982 Dr. Gallin argues that "by subjugating the interests of women to those of men — and theoretically the interests of the young to those of the old — the family perpetuates dependencies that serve the needs and interests of the state."

"To gain economic and social security in old age," the author continues, "mothers-in-law must assume some of the role responsibilities of their daughters-in-law, thereby supplying industry with the labor force it needs to survive in the international market economy. To secure their futures, daughters-in-law must assume responsibility for the physical needs of their mothers-in-law, thereby obviating governmental expenditure on welfare assistance for the aged."

"The accommodation of women's mutual dependence maintains and reaffirms the ideology of patriarchal familism needed by the government to justify the employment practices and underdeveloped social security system that underpin [Taiwan's export-oriented] political economy."

Gidwani, Sushila. *Impact of Monetary and Financial Policies Upon Women.* UN International Research and Training Institute for the Advancement of Women (INSTRAW). *Research Study,* no. 1, May 1985. 44pp. References, statistical tables.

Dr. Gidwani's study of women and international monetary and financial policies opens with a brief description of the policies themselves and the role of women in international economic affairs (in the preagricultural, agricultural, and industrial ages). The study then moves to a detailed analysis of the impact of the monetary system and monetary policies upon women. "More and more women," the author notes, "are shifting from unpaid domestic production to the paid market production." "What role," she asks, "have money and monetary policies played in this pattern of transition?" And what price have women paid in making this shift?

The present economic environment for women, Dr. Gidwani concludes, "mirrors the economic environment for men in the early stages of industrial development of the advanced countries." "However," she adds, "unlike the old days where colonies and the Americas provided an outlet for growth and unemployment, the present nations, devoid of colonies and faced with an extremely competitive environment, have recourse only to economic growth and/or to income and wealth redistribution measures." The latter, she explains, is the only course that offers any hope to women.

This study closes with some challenging ideas about an alternative "to the present totally male-oriented system" and a five-page bibliography.

Guatemala History Told by Its Women. Trans. Women for Guatemala. Available also from Guatemala News and Information Bureau (Oakland, Calif.). 1983. 24pp. $1.50. Notes.

This booklet contains the testimony of Guatemalan women presented to the People's Permanent Tribunal concerning "the constant and systematic violation of human rights in Guatemala [under the government of Gen. Efraín Ríos Montt]." Their formal denunciation is based on "testimonies which give evidence of the campaign of indiscriminate demolition practiced by the Guatemalan army, constituting government massacres of the people in the countryside, and kidnapping and murder in the city."

The brutal violence visited upon women in Guatemala and the terrible burdens they bear are graphically described in the personal testimonies and case histories of more than fifteen women. "In each case," reads the introduction, "the strength and clarity of women stands out. At no time do their accounts show signs of weakness. Each of them relies on her enormous struggling spirit and responsibility in the decisions that she has made."

Industrial Women Workers in Asia. **Committee for Asian Women and Isis International.** *Isis International Women's Journal,* **no. 4. Sept. 1985. 160pp. $4. Feature articles, illustrations, charts, diagrams, photographs, statistical tables, notes, bibliography, list of resources.**

This collection of twelve articles written by nine Asian women researchers and organizers is a major contribution to our understanding of the complex situation of industrial women workers in the capitalist countries of Asia. The impact of industrialization on women, strategies and prospects for organizing women workers, the role of women in trade unions, gender subordination and sexual discrimination at work — these and many other subjects are treated in well-documented fashion.

An annotated bibliography of print and audiovisual materials on working women completes this invaluable handbook.

Jaquette, Jane S. *Women Food Producers: Potential Power for Combating World Hunger.* **OEF International. 1985. 28pp. $5, surface postage included. Case studies, report findings, action suggestions, lists of resources, bibliography, references.**

Written in accessible, nontechnical language this attractive primer on women and world hunger uses brief case studies from a variety of Third World countries to dramatize the gap that exists "between the work women actually do in agriculture — the growing, processing, and storing of food — and their 'visibility' to policymakers . . ." In Africa, writes the president of OEF International in his introduction, "60 to 80 percent of the agricultural work is done by women. Until recently, however, African men were the primary targets of foreign assistance programs providing technical training or improved agricultural inputs."

Dr. Jaquette describes solutions that would increase the access women have to agricultural resources and give them greater control over the results of their own labor. "Attempts to solve the problem of world hunger," she concludes, "cannot be separated from the recognition of women's roles as food producers."

The booklet gives a progress report on initiatives already in the works, offers action suggestions, and lists organizational, print, and audiovisual resources on this subject.

The Cummins Engine Foundation gave its financial support to the publication of *Women Food Producers.*

Lives of Working Women in India. **Selected readings from** *Manushi: A Journal about Women and Society, 1979–1980.* **21pp. $1.50. Available from the Women's International Resource Exchange. Articles (reproduced), illustrations, photographs.**

Three of the five pieces in this collection of articles from India's leading women's journal provide intimate insights into the daily work lives of the "unclean" who sweep the streets of India's cities, the women who do the unskilled and semiskilled labor in India's coal mines, and of the *hamal* women who transport various kinds of goods on their heads or by handcarts to and from railway stations. Complementing those three articles are brief reports on two significant women's movements in India: a legendary upsurge of sharecropping peasants in Bengal during 1946–50 (the "Tebhaga Movement") and the Mahila Samta Sainik Dal, a militant feminist organization of college students in Maharashtra.

Longwe, Sara Hlupekile. *Legalized Discrimination against Women in Zambia.* **Women in International Development, Michigan State University.** *Working Papers on Women in International Development,* **no. 102, 1985. 19pp. $2.50. Notes.**

Stimulated by a personal experience of discrimination against women, Sara Longwe sought to determine whether such discrimination existed only in administrative practice and in defiance of the law or whether the law itself was discriminatory. Her study confirmed the fact that while the constitution of Zambia does offer protection on grounds of tribe and race, "there is no general protection against discrimination based on sex."

Longwe, co-secretary of the Zambia Association for Research and Development in Lusaka, considers examples of legalized discrimination against women in the Employment Act and in the Income Tax Act. She also describes some examples of discrimination in the government's administrative practice in such areas as women's access to credit facilities, extension services, and education.

Legalized Discrimination concludes with a brief consideration of actions that Zambian women must take "collectively" to ensure that discriminatory laws and practices are changed.

Lycette, Margaret A. *Improving Women's Access to Credit in the Third World: Policy and Project Recommendations.* **International Center for Research on Women.** *ICRW Occasional Paper,* **no. 1, June 1984. 28pp. $5. References, bibliography, appendix.**

This Ford Foundation–sponsored study searches for ways to improve access to financial credit "for the large proportion of women in developing countries who, unable to afford either unemployment or very low paid formal-sector jobs, operate as traders and small-scale entrepreneurs in the informal sector."

The paper analyzes the obstacles that exist now—from the point of view of the women-as-borrowers and the financial institutions—and describes the ways in which women meet their credit needs "through informal sources of finance such as relatives and friends, moneylenders, pawnbrokers, and informal rotating savings associations."

The author concludes with a number of policy and project-level reforms that she believes will improve women's access to formal finance while incorporating the desirable features of the existing informal systems.

McCarthy, Florence E., and Shelley Feldman. *Rural Women Discovered: New Sources of Capital and Labor in Bangladesh.* **Women in Inter-**

national Development, Michigan State University. *Working Papers on Women in International Development,* no. 105, 1985. 23pp. $2.75. Notes, statistical tables, references.

In analyzing the effects of capitalist penetration in Bangladesh the authors of this study challenge two current models of progressive thinking on development: the development-underdevelopment approach advanced by André Gunder Frank and the world-systems model popularized by Immanuel Wallerstein. McCarthy and Feldman state their case effectively and persuasively, concentrating their attention particularly on the incorporation of rural women into development processes in Bangladesh.

"Rural women," the authors demonstrate, "are being forced to join the labor force because of worsening socio-economic conditions in the country. This has the potential for providing cheap sources of labor in the rural areas with the additional potential of lowering wage rates and enhancing the competition among rural laborers."

The authors arrive at three policy interpretations: (1) "the current regime [in Bangladesh], and the international donor community, have been forced to alter and diversify standard development agendas in order to stimulate sectors of the economy and engage the participation of people once ignored by development programs"; (2) foreign aid and other programs directed at women and the dispossessed avoid prescriptions for political transformation and "have little to do with issues of equity or fundamental social reform"; and (3) "conceptions of what are suitable activities for women or assumptions about their intellectual capacities are incorporated into training and credit programs."

McLean, Scilla, Stella Efua Graham, et al. *Female Circumcision, Excision, and Infibulation.* **Minority Rights Group.** *MRG Report,* no. 47, July 1985. 2nd rev. ed. 21pp. $3.95. Map, illustrations, notes, references, list of resources.

Genital mutilations affect "several tens of millions of women" in Africa, the Middle East, and other areas of the Third World. The practice, according to the evidence presented in this report, is "medically unnecessary, painful, and [an] extremely dangerous operation."

In a detailed and sensitive style this MRG report endeavors to communicate the facts about female genital mutilation, drawing on information from many countries in Africa, and then to discuss practical programs to eradicate the custom. The recommended actions, the editors say, are "limited to proposals which can be put into operation immediately, given goodwill in the countries concerned, and given practical and financial assistance from international organisations."

Malahleha, Gwendoline Mphokho. *Contradictions and Ironies: Women of Lesotho.* **Change International Reports,** no. 13, n.d. 12pp. $3. Map, diagrams, statistical tables, bibliography.

Contradictions and Ironies examines the situation of women in the tiny, mountainous country of Lesotho. Completely surrounded by the Republic of South Africa, Lesotho has long served South Africa as a grain source and a labor reserve. These two factors have had a tremendous effect on the position of Basotho women ("Basotho" is the collective name for the inhabitants of Lesotho).

Contrary to images of African society as unchanging and tradition-bound, this report describes how "Basotho women have had to develop a great deal of self-reliance and initiative in managing household, community, and national affairs." In rural areas particularly, women have had to shoulder enormous burdens as the men have migrated in search of employment either in urban areas within Lesotho or in South Africa.

Newland, Kathleen. *Women, Men, and the Division of Labor.* Worldwatch Institute. *Worldwatch Paper,* no. 37, May 1980. 44pp. $2.

The age-old division that places most men in paid labor and most women in unpaid work is breaking down, according to the author of this study. "Nearly half the world's adult women are in the labor force," Newland states, "a category that excludes women who do only unpaid work at home."

One issue is still untouched, says the author: "the sharing of unpaid household labor between women and men receives only a fraction of the attention given to equality in formal employment." "If women are to take full advantage of newly won access to the formal labor market," writes the author of *The Sisterhood of Man* (New York: W. W. Norton, 1979), "men must increase their share of the essential work that goes on outside of it [i.e., in the home]. Otherwise, equal opportunity for women will turn out to be a recipe for overwork."

Newland examines the impact of reforms in this situation in Peru and describes actions that the government of Sweden has taken regarding the division of labor.

Nicaraguan Women: Unlearning the Alphabet of Submission. Women's International Resource Exchange. Fall 1985. 46pp. $3. Translated articles, interviews, charts, photographs, list of resources, appendix.

This selection of articles, interviews, poetry, and reprinted editorials covers women in agriculture in Nicaragua, the Sandinista philosophy of government, the family, women's leadership, prostitutes in Nicaragua, native peoples, self-transformation, and the human and material costs of the U.S.-backed war against Nicaragua.

In one article U.S. feminist Adrienne Rich records her thoughts on the interface between women's struggles in Nicaragua and Euro-North American philosophies of women's liberation. "I came home from Nicaragua," she writes, "convinced that white feminists need to keep defining and describing our relationship both to capitalism and socialism and to talk seriously about our place in the interconnecting movements for bread, self-determination, dignity, and justice."

Nicaraguan Women and the Revolution. Women's International Resource Exchange, 1982, rev. ed. 32pp. $2.50. Articles (reproduced), poetry, illustrations, photographs, statistical tables.

This collection includes articles from *Barricada* (Managua, Nicaragua), *Isis International Bulletin, Nicaraguan Perspectives, Guardian*

(New York), and *Mujer: Revolución,* a special publication of AMNLAE, the women's association of Nicaragua. One-half of the publication is given to the poems of Gioconda Belli, Olivia Silva, and Claribel Alegría.

The articles and poetry all deal with the legacy of discrimination and inequality that revolutionary Nicaragua inherited from the Somoza regime. "All these problems," Commander Tomás Borge says in one selection, "a legacy of the unjust society of the past, are gradually being confronted by our revolution. We made the revolution so that we could confront and resolve these problems [of injustices toward women]. As our country develops we will resolve the material problems; we will build more daycare centers, more public laundries, community dining rooms; we will create better work opportunities."

Borge stresses that there is a need for personal transformation as well: "It is the task of both men and women to struggle against old attitudes, inherited prejudices and customs, which place women in a double situation of oppression." "Some day," he concludes, "our women will have won the legitimate right to equality. And on that day, we men will be freer. The day that justice is truly done to women, on that day we men will be happier. On the day which sees true equality of women, society will have won the most beautiful of battles."

North-South Institute. *Women and International Development Cooperation: Trade and Investment.* **UN International Research and Training Institute for the Advancement of Women (INSTRAW).** *Research Study,* **no. 1-G, May 1985. 52pp. References, statistical tables, bibliography.**

This study, prepared by the North-South Institute in Canada, demonstrates that women "frequently have not benefited from economic development to the same extent as men." "In some cases," the report states, "there is evidence that women's situation is actually becoming worse and that they have experienced a disproportionate share of the dislocation that usually accompanies economic change and development."

The study opens with an overview of selected trade and development trends and then analyzes their implications for women's employment in various sectors and industries in developing countries. The authors examine two industries in detail: the electronics industry and the textile and clothing industry.

Three pages of "directions for action" and a four-page bibliography bring the study to a close.

O'Brien, Patricia J. *Population Policy, Economic Development, and Multinational Corporations in Latin America.* **Women in International Development, Michigan State University.** *Working Papers on Women in International Development,* **no. 32, 1983. 30pp. $3.**

For many years, this study notes, social scientists have debated various ideological positions on the population-development issue. What has been absent from these discussions, however, is "the role played by multinational corporations in perpetuating both adverse population processes and economic underdevelopment in Third World countries."

The author, a university professor of sociology, first examines the impact of this neglected dimension as it relates to an understanding of the structural crisis of Latin American countries. Second, she analyzes the impact of multinational corporations on Latin American women and how the globalization of capital undermines some widely accepted propositions concerning the role of women in economic development. Finally, Professor O'Brien describes the impact of multinational corporations on internal migration pressures.

"There are structural tendencies inherent in the present global economy," this report concludes, "that perpetuate economic underdevelopment. To the extent that population policies aimed at containing population growth and directing population distribution are often adopted in response to such underdevelopment, it is not surprising that they are less than adequate as a national response to a global problem."

Our Rightful Share. **Committee for Asian Women, CCA-URM. 1984. 112pp. $3. Cartoon illustrations, statistical tables, references.**

In the style of the ". . . for Beginners" books that have become popular in recent years this booklet presents a cartoon history of the growth and effects of labor legislation and women workers in Asia. "Viewed from the side of the women workers in Asia," the editors write, "*Our Rightful Share* seeks to examine the effectiveness of the [International Labour Office] Conventions, promulgated to protect the interest of the working class, by exposing the violations of these conventions . . ." The booklet covers the growth of the female labor force in Asia, and specific topics such as wages, night work, maternity leave, the right to organize, and the right to strike.

Though very much an organizing tool by and for women workers in Asia, *Our Rightful Share* is a powerful educational resource for persons outside the region who desire to understand better and more effectively support the struggle of Asia's women workers.

Our Stories: Lives of Filipina Women. **Synapses. February 1985. 8pp. Stories, illustrations.**

This sampling of women's stories and poems from the Philippines comes from a seventy-page compilation done originally by the Center for Women Resources in Manila, Philippines.

"Many of us have no experience in public speaking," the women say at the start, "nor have we been written about. But we believe in our capacity to create spirals of insights. We long to release our stored whispers, our songs of woe, our poems of struggle."

The excerpts in this leaflet are from a forty-year-old peasant woman, an apparel worker at the Mariveles export processing zone, a labor organizer, a tribal woman from Panay, and others.

The Plight of Asian Workers in Electronics. **Illustrations by Porise Lo. Christian Conference of Asia-Urban Rural Mission. October 1982. 85pp. $2. Cartoon illustrations, photographs, statistical tables.**

"This is the story of over 600,000 workers in Asia," this booklet begins. "Eighty percent of [them] are young women, mostly aged between 15 and 25. All of them are employed in the electronics industry — the technologically most advanced industry in the modern world."

In five chapters and in engaging cartoon style *Plight* tells us about these women workers, how they are being exploited, by whom, why Asian governments accommodate the electronics multinationals, and what actions have been and can be taken to transform present conditions.

Rakowski, Cathy A. *Women in Nontraditional Industry: The Case of Steel in Ciudad Guayana, Venezuela.* Women in International Development, Michigan State University. *Working Papers on Women in International Development,* no. 104, 1985. 23pp. $2.75. Notes, bibliography.

This paper describes the incorporation of women into heavy industry in and around Ciudad Guayana, site of the large-scale Venezuelan Guayana Development Program, during the employment boom of 1974–1979 and the decline in female employment in the years thereafter.

The first two sections of *Women in Nontraditional Industry* outline the features of the incorporation of women into the workforce at a specialty steel plant and at the state-owned steel mill which, combined, account for over 70 percent of all manufacturing employment in the city.

The third section describes the discrimination that two groups of women, laborers and engineers, faced at the plant and the mill.

The final section analyzes the effects of discrimination on worker behavior and suggests that both male discriminatory behavior and female coping mechanisms are not only the result of the structural factors of power, opportunity, and numbers identified in previous studies, but are also associated with factors of class, age, and culture. These latter factors are "important to the development or implementation of corrective programs designed to increase productivity and to overcome discrimination as a factor adversely affecting productivity in a particular organization or culture."

Retrenchment! Committee for Asian Women. *Asian Women Workers Newsletter* 4, no. 3 (Dec. 1985). 12pp. $1. Illustrations, editorial, news reports, list of resources.

This issue of the CAW newsletter features reports and analyses of the layoffs and plant shutdowns that have plagued Asian workers in recent years. *Retrenchment!* also describes union activities in the Philippines, Japan, and China and discusses job prospects for women in South Korea and India.

The editorial weighs the implications of "retrenchment" for women workers. "Whenever choices have to be made about who is to be retrenched and who is to remain, it is always the women to be retrenched and the men to remain." The reasons are not surprising: "women are still viewed primarily as wives and mothers" (thus they constitute a "reserve army" that "can be moved in and out of the workforce in accordance with the changing demand for labor") and women workers are still largely unskilled (thus "the opportunity cost for laying them off is small when compared to that of well-trained male technicians").

Rouse, Shahnaz J. *Women's Movements in Contemporary Pakistan: Results and Prospects.* **Women in International Development, Michigan State University.** *Working Papers on Women in International Development,* no. 74, 1984. 24pp. $2.75. Notes, references.

"Women in Pakistan," writes the author of this WID report, "are the victims of various types of repression and oppression. Women as well as men suffer from being part of a socio-economic framework dominated by international capital in which their contributions and status are often determined by forces external to themselves. Within this framework, however, women are further oppressed because they belong to the gender that is seen as necessary for maintenance of the system, but is relatively unrecognized and poorly rewarded for its contribution to that maintenance." "Women are victimized," Rouse concludes, "not only by the economic system but also by the dominant social relations within it."

After analyzing these and other factors that combine to explain the situation of women in Pakistan today, the author concludes that (1) an integration of the women's questions with a total transformation of social relations becomes an absolute necessity; and (2) it is essential that "women retain an independent organization so that their cause does not become subservient to other issues."

Second Latin American and Caribbean Feminist Meeting, Lima, Peru. **Isis International, with Organizing Collective of the Second Meeting.** *Isis International Women's Journal,* no. 1, 1984. 82pp. $4. Photographs, illustrations, list of resources, appendixes.

Six hundred women from all over Latin America and the Caribbean came together in Lima, Peru, in July 1983 to participate in the Second Latin American and Caribbean Feminist Meeting. (The first took place in Bogotá, Colombia, in 1981). This inaugural issue of the *Women's Journal,* produced at the then newly opened Isis office in Santiago, reports on the conference and on "the whole range of issues women are mobilizing around in Latin America [and] the problems and difficulties we women are facing not only in our situations but in the women's movement itself."

The bulk of the well-designed booklet is given to reports on twenty-one conference workshops. Each report opens with a summary of the question posed and addressed. This is followed by a two- to three-page summary of the discussions in the workshop. Topics covered included health, church, family, peasant women, violence and sexual slavery, older women, literature, and racism.

Three appendixes provide: (1) "Resolutions and Motions of the Second Meeting," (2) "Motions made at the Plenary of the Second Meeting," and (3) "Resources: Papers, Publications, and Audiovisuals."

Sivard, Ruth Leger. *Women: A World Survey.* **World Priorities. 1985. 44pp. $5. Maps, illustrations, statistical tables, notes, glossary, chronology.**

Put a renowned author and research analyst together with the financial backing from the Carnegie Corporation and the Ford and Rockefeller Foundations and you are certain to wind up with a classy product. Such is the case with this world survey: glossy cover, full color throughout, attractive maps, tables, and diagrams, abundant sidebar material, and obviously well-researched text.

Sivard, who is perhaps best known as the author of the annual *World Military and Social Expenditures,* defines her task in this survey as bringing together "in an easily accessible and abbreviated form a range of factual information on the situation of women in the world community today." "To give perspective to the picture," she adds, "the focus is on changes which have occurred since World War II." These changes, Sivard concludes, have been extremely uneven and, on the whole, modest.

Women: A World Survey covers women's work, education, and health, among many other subjects. This is a highly recommended resource for group or individual study.

Stern, Brigitte. *The Changing Role of Women in International Economic Relations.* **UN International Research and Training Institute for the Advancement of Women (INSTRAW).** *Research Studies,* **no. 1-A, June 1985. 56pp. Notes, statistical tables, appendixes.**

"Women are central — and not marginal — in the development process," writes the author of this INSTRAW study. "Women have to be active, not passive, in the development process."

Dr. Brigitte Stern, of the University of Paris X, sets the context for women's active involvement in development by describing the international economic structures within which women function (part 1), the present situation of women in international economic relations (part 2), and, finally, the steps that can be taken to enhance the involvement of women in shaping the new international economic order (part 3).

"Women's issues," the author concludes, "cannot be considered as specific issues to be solved in addition to and/or after other general economic issues that are deemed more urgent and important . . . Women must not be treated as a specific, underprivileged group, but as a part — and in fact a major part — of the world's population." This study is Dr. Stern's contribution to the "permanent transformation in the present socioeconomic system" that she contends will ultimately benefit women as well as men.

Tiano, Susan. *Maquiladoras, Women's Work, and Unemployment in Northern Mexico.* **Women in International Development, Michigan State University.** *Working Papers on Women in International Development,* **no. 43, 1984. 32pp. $3. Notes, references, statistical tables.**

Although Mexico's Border Industrialization Program (BIP) was initiated to relieve unemployment in northern cities, critics claim that it has not served this end. Many analysts have claimed that the main reason for this failure is that unemployment in northern Mexico, as in the nation as a whole, is a male problem, yet women constitute the bulk of the BIP workforce.

In this WID research study, Susan Tiano, an assistant professor of sociology at the University of New Mexico, gathers aggregate data on men's and women's labor force participation to demonstrate that that claim is based on several inaccurate assumptions. Average unemployment rates, for instance, are shown to be higher among women than men of comparable ages throughout the nation. Furthermore, joblessness is pronounced among younger women—that sector of the labor force from which the majority of BIP workers are recruited.

Dr. Tiano's conclusion is that the BIP does not appear to have enhanced women's labor-market situation relative to men's. Rather, she maintains, "the same conditions which weaken women's employment status in other parts of Mexico also operate in the North, despite any job opportunities the program might offer." The author draws upon propositions from Marxist-feminist theory to interpret these empirical trends.

Maquiladoras are assembly-line workers in foreign-owned plants in northern Mexico.

Tien, H. Yuan. *Redirection of the Chinese Family: Ramifications of Minimal Reproduction.* **Women in International Development, Michigan State University.** *Working Papers on Women in International Development,* **no. 67, 1984. 13pp. $2.25. Notes.**

In this short paper Ohio State University's H. Yuan Tien goes beyond a simple cost-benefit analysis of the Chinese government's attempts to end the country's "reproductive anarchy" and poses behavioral and sociological questions that he believes have to be "considered with much more imagination and foresight."

"The policy of minimal reproduction creates new circumstances for marriage," Dr. Tien states. "Women will be able to fulfill the tasks of childbearing and childrearing in a relatively short span of time. What will women be doing after completing the minimal reproduction? With time on their hands, will women be more able to contemplate and conduct their lives in different terms?"

"Furthermore," he asks, "what will be the nature of married life?" With sex and reproduction separated, "will there emerge the view that sex can be for pleasure only? If so, will women be more able to emphasize love and romance in their relationships with men?"

To Honour Women's Day: Profiles of Leading Women in the South African and Namibian Liberation Struggles. **International Defence and Aid Fund for Southern Africa, in cooperation with the United Nations Centre against Apartheid. August 1981. 56pp. £1. Biographies, photographs, glossary, annotated list of women political prisoners in South Africa and Namibia. Available in North America from IDAF, P.O. Box 17, Cambridge, MA 02238 and the Africa Resource Center, 464 19 St., Oakland, CA 94612. $2.50, postage included.**

On the twenty-fifth anniversary of the day in August 1956 when twenty thousand women from all over South Africa gathered in Pretoria to condemn the government's extension of the despised "pass laws" to women, the IDAF and the UN Centre against Apartheid published this booklet describing the lives and experiences of some thirty women who "have all made outstanding contributions to the struggle for a free, democratic, and non-racial Southern Africa." "All have endured personal hardship and suffering under apartheid," the editors write in the introduction. "They have been banned, detained, tortured, imprisoned, driven into exile or have experienced other forms of victimisation."

The one- and two-page biographies in this booklet are of women who were selected as being representative "of all the women who, throughout South Africa and Namibia, are carrying forward the banner of the freedom struggle in the townships, the houses, farms, and factories of their employers, the regime's prisons and detention camps, in the bantustans, and from places of exile throughout the world."

Voices of Women: Poetry by and about Third World Women. **Women's International Resource Exchange. November 1982. $2.50. Illustrations, photographs, references.**

"No women have more reason to reclaim their history, their cultural heritage, than the women of the Third World and the women of color in the United States," declares the introduction to *Voices of Women.* "Denied as women," the introduction continues, "denied as persons of color, denied as producers of the world's goods, denied as citizens of countries whose own autonomy is denied by the Western ruling powers, theirs is a rich legacy waiting to be discovered, to serve as a map for the paths that women everywhere are traversing in the search for affirmation, for identity, for empowerment."

This anthology of forty-two poems by and about Third World women begins to redress the imbalance the WIRE collective describes in the introduction: "Standard poetry anthologies have, for the most part, provided little evidence that Third World women have lived, that they have written of their history of pain and travail, of survival and assertion, little evidence that they are today demanding their rightful role in those struggles of their people which can—if women are present in them—lead to fuller, more creative, more autonomous lives for women, indeed for everyone."

We Continue Forever: Sorrow and Strength of Guatemalan Women. **Women's International Resource Exchange. 1983. 58pp. $3. Map, illustrations, photographs, reprinted articles, interviews, poetry, list of resources. Available also in Spanish:** *Siempre vamos: Angustia y valentía de la mujer guatemalteca.*

This WIRE anthology includes a number of excerpts from J. L. Fried et al., eds., *Guatemala in Rebellion* (New York: Grove Press, 1983), along with documents from the guerrilla movement and women's organizations in Guatemala, poetry, and interviews with Isabel Fraire, a Mexican-born poet and literary critic and with three indigenous women and two women organizers.

The booklet also contains a lengthy "testimony" from María Lupe, one of the first compañeras to join the guerrilla resistance in the early 1970s. She describes her personal history, the movement's patient attempts to bring the non-Indian Guatemalan peasants into the revolutionary struggle, and the efforts of both women and men in the movement to go about their work in a non-discriminatory manner.

Weiss, Anita M. *Women in Pakistan: Implications of the Current Program of Islamization.* **Women in International Development, Michigan State University.** *Working Papers on Women in International Development,* **no. 78, 1985. 23pp. $2.75. Notes, bibliography.**

This pamphlet is concerned with the current position of women in Pakistan, focusing particularly on the changes that the Pakistani government's program of Islamization has had and may have on women's lives. After providing some background on Islamic legal theory and the historical conflict of interpretation of that theory in South Asia, the author—a professor of sociology at the University of California-Berkeley—addresses the relationship between the new Islamic laws (both decreed and proposed) and women's position in Pakistan.

Dr. Weiss analyzes the implications of—and reasons for—the government's program of *nizam-i-islam,* an attempt to bring all laws in Pakistan into conformity with Islamic tenets and values. She weighs the program's impact on women and on the social environment it is designed to shape and describes the variety of responses to the government's program.

Woman to Woman. New Internationalist, **nos. 149 and 150, July and August 1985. Feature articles, photographs, illustrations, statistical tables, diagrams, lists of resources, charts.**

The first issue in this two-volume set contains an adaptation of the report on the state of the world's women that the staff of *New Internationalist* prepared in response to a request from the United Nations (*Women: A World Report*). To mark the end of the United Nations Decade for Women (1975–1985) *New Internationalist* invited ten leading women writers—five from the rich world, five from the poor world—to take part in an international exchange, with Third World writers going to the rich world and writers from Australia, England, Norway, and the United States going to Third World countries. Edited by Debbie Taylor, this issue presents the results of the exchange, covering topics such as the family, agriculture, health, sex, education, and politics.

Edited by Amada Root, the second issue in the series discusses the ways in which feminism "aims to change men's, women's, and children's lives: from their most intimate and loving moments to the organisation of work and political power." With its customary attention to attractive design and engaging illustrations the magazine presents articles and statistical material on equal pay and work opportunities for women, equal rights, sexual freedom, the intimate connection between politics and personal life, and men's control of public life.

Specifically Third World-related aspects of these issues are treated by Rachael Grossman (women workers in Malaysia's electronics industry) and Buchi Emecheta (women's lives in America and Africa).

Women: A Dynamic Dimension in Development. UN International Research and Training Institute for the Advancement of Women (INSTRAW). *Policy Paper,* no. 2, June 1985. 20pp. Free. Notes.

Though addressed primarily to United Nations staff and burdened with official UN verbiage this short pamphlet is, nevertheless, a concise and useful statement of how "incorporating women's needs and concerns in development policies and plans lends a new dynamic dimension to development."

After situating the "women in development" issue within the UN's legislative mandate and underlining the fact that women "are already full participants in development" (but lack a voice in development *planning*), the booklet then proceeds to a sectorial analysis of women's roles in agriculture; water supply and sanitation; energy; and industry. In all cases, the writers conclude, women are "usually overlooked in planning for development, in that they are not viewed as direct agents and beneficiaries of the development process."

Women and Health. Women and Development Unit, University of the West Indies. *Woman Speak!,* no. 9, December/January 1983. 28pp. Articles, news reports, illustrations, photographs.

"Women comprise half the total world population," the editors of *Woman Speak!* remind us. "The health and well-being of their families rest mainly with them, since they are responsible for the nurturing, feeding, and treatment of minor illnesses of their children and other household members. The status of their health, then, affects the health of present and future generations."

This issue of *Woman Speak!* highlights some of the areas of health that bear directly on women and the contribution they make to the development of their societies. Topics covered include reproduction, family planning, nutrition, occupational safety and health, breastfeeding, mental health, and fatigue. Running through many of the articles is the observation that women are far removed from the decision-making processes of health care systems and medical research, but that they do play a major role in primary health care at the community level.

Women and Militarism. Peoples Translation Service. *Connexions,* no. 11, Winter 1984. 32pp. $3. Translated feature articles, advertisements, book reviews, poetry, illustrations, photographs, list of resources.

Worldwide there have been only twenty-six days without battle since the end of World War II, and all of these days fell in September 1945. Since 1945 there have been 150 wars. An average of eleven wars are fought each year.

The editors of this issue of *Connexions* call these grim realities to our attention by way of introduction to this more particular study of how militarism affects women's lives, how women suffer from war, and how they perpetuate it.

"Militarism," they write, "is a deeply embedded, ongoing set of processes which operate long before and long after actual battles are fought. Women's role is often portrayed as secondary to the serious business of soldiering. However, without women's participation, the institution of militarism would come to a grinding halt." "Once we recognize the active roles that women play," the editors conclude, "then we can begin to see the many possible ways that militarism can be challenged."

Contributions to this collection from the Third World deal with the destruction of the social and economic structures surrounding U.S. military bases overseas, armed resistance to Israeli occupation of the West Bank, the continuing struggle of women freedom fighters in Zimbabwe (against discrimination in the new society), the role of the new majority of women in Kampuchea, the tragic war between Iran and Iraq, and women in the beleaguered nations of Central America.

Women and Politics. **Middle East Research and Information Project (MERIP).** *MERIP Middle East Report* **16, no. 1 (Jan.–Feb. 1986). 48pp. $3.50/£2.50. Feature articles, editorial, comment and analysis, interview, updates, documents, reviews, photographs, list of publications received, notes, advertisements.**

The four major articles in this issue present an analysis of the nature of women's roles in the public sphere (state policy) and the domestic sphere (kin and community) that is unique in Middle East studies. In his introductory remarks Suad Joseph notes that "the discourse of public/domestic domains in the study of Middle East women has been relatively static, compared with feminist studies of other regions." By contrast, he says, the articles in *Women and Politics* "give accounts of fluid, shifting relationships. The boundaries are neither fixed nor irreversible. The state expands and retreats, kin and communal groups gain and lose control over members. Women's location and the definition of their activities shift as the boundaries move, or as they become more or less permeable."

Author Judith Tucker argues that as the Egyptian state developed, formal politics expanded and women's participation declined ("Insurrectionary Women: Women and the State in 19th Century Egypt"); Mary Hegland observes that the strengthening of the state in Iran under the shah reduced local political factionalism and competition, an arena where women had been active ("Political Roles of Iranian Village Women"); Julie Peteet finds that among Palestinian women, politics has become an integral part of domesticity ("No Going Back: Women and the Palestinian Movement"); and Sondra Hale explains how the separation of public and domestic has been harmful to women in Sudan and argues that the reintegration of the two spheres would increase women's rights ("The Wing of the Patriarch: Sudanese Women and Revolutionary Parties").

Women and Prostitution. **Peoples Translation Service.** *Connexions,* **no. 12, Spring 1984. 32pp. $3. Translated feature articles, advertisements, illustrations, photographs, references, list of resources.**

"We see prostitutes as workers," write the editors of this issue of *Con-*

nexions, "and, like most workers, their job is difficult and often unpleasant. We asked ourselves why women become prostitutes and looked to them for answers." The answers presented in *Women and Prostitution* come from women all around the world, from Italy to Australia, from Peru to Pakistan.

Admitting that they came to this issue with ambivalence and biases the editors, nevertheless, reached the conclusion that "prostitutes should not be blamed because prostitution is their means of support. Prostitution exists because of economic and sexual double standards which result in low pay for women and high unemployment. Our anger and our criticism are directed against the social systems that support abusive prostitution, and not against prostitutes."

Articles that treat prosititution in Third World countries come from publications in Thailand, Chile, Peru, Zimbabwe, Pakistan, and Mexico.

Women in a Changing World. Cultural Survival. *Cultural Survival Quarterly,* **1984. 80pp. $2. Feature articles, photographs, references, bibliographies, statistical tables. Available also in Spanish in an abbreviated format:** *La Mujer y el cambio.*

"While it is difficult to generalize about the current situation of women in the thousands of ethnic groups in the world," write the editors, "this issue [of *Cultural Survival Quarterly*] identifies some apparent trends. The articles that follow—as well as a number of other publications, some of which are listed in this issue—indicate that with a few exceptions the plight of tribal or ethnically distinct women is worse than that of men."

Believing that an evaluation of the relationship of a woman's culture to that of dominant cultures or politico-economic systems may give insights into "the diverse problems that confront women in the world," the editors present this collection of succinct studies of women in the following contexts: women of groups in initial contact with dominant cultures or systems; women of groups in sustained contact with these cultures or systems; women and state policies and programs; women and industries; and women and the political arena.

The well-documented articles in this collection and the many supplementary recommended readings offer ample documentation in support of the editors' conclusions that "as societies come into increasing contact with larger economic and political systems, the lives of women are irrevocably altered, in many cases negatively. Yet, improvements in the lives of these women can only be brought about within the context of their own cultures and within the cultures of the groups that are coming to dominate them."

Women's Human Rights Denied. Amnesty International U.S.A. 1985. Free. Photographs.

This well-designed nine-panel leaflet would be an excellent handout for study groups concerned about the "silencing" of women around the world, through detention, banning, and murder. The leaflet provides capsule summaries (from reports available to Amnesty International as of October 1983) of the cases of individual women, such as Winnie Mandela (South Africa), Kongit Kebede (Ethiopia), Marianela García Villas (El Salvador), and Lu Hsiu-Lien (Taiwan), as well as of the Mothers of the Plaza de Mayo (Argentina) and the women and children incarcerated in Iran's Zendan-e Zanan (Women's Prison).

These women, the introduction states, "are victims of intimidation, illegal arrest and detention, and torture by governmental and paragovernmental agents. They are victims of official campaigns to deny human rights and to crush the human spirit."

Women's Movements: Thoughts into Action. **Peoples Translation Service.** *Connexions,* **no. 19, Winter 1986. 32pp. $3.75. Translated feature articles, advertisements, illustrations, photographs, references, list of resources.**

"Although women's priorities do differ around the world," write the editors of *Women's Movements,* "some of the fundamental struggles that women have been and are presently engaged in have points in common." These points are reflected in the diversity of the subjects of the articles included in this issue of *Connexions:* organizing against the dictatorships in Chile and Pakistan, documenting the situation of women in Nigeria and in Iran, racism in the women's movement in Canada, dissatisfaction with collectivist work in the Netherlands, and developments in the vital women's organizations in the Philippines and in Latin America/Caribbean.

Two common themes that emerge from this diversity, the editors conclude, "are the need for autonomous organizations that have links to other social movements, and the conflicts caused by divisions of race, class, sexuality, religion, and ethnicity."

Recognizing these difficulties within the movement and noting that women's access to media and communication is "still limited," the editors, nevertheless, rejoice in the breakthough they have witnessed (and, indeed, have contributed to) in women's networking both regionally and internationally. As evidence they cite the growth in their own resource lists and the more than doubling of participants at the two United Nations conferences that began and ended the Decade for Women: 6,000 in Mexico City in 1975 and over 13,000 in Nairobi in 1985.

Women's Words. **Peoples Translation Service.** *Connexions,* **no. 13, Summer 1984. 32pp. $3. Translated feature articles, advertisements, book reviews, illustrations, photographs, references, list of resources.**

"Women have not been silent," write the editors of this issue of *Connexions.* "In their songs, proverbs and tales, the history and traditions of whole cultures have been preserved. Their words have filled diaries and letters, novels, plays and speeches—even the news shared between neighbors that binds a community together has echoed the ring of women's voices."

"And yet," the editors note, "as in so many areas of women's experience, the recognition and validation of the 'public' world has been long in coming. Women's words have been circumscribed by illiteracy, by charges of being too 'personal' or 'subjective' for inclusion in the realm of Literature, by time, space and economic limitations, and by the whole constellation of social institutions and technology that has closed against them."

This summer 1984 issue of *Connexions* gives voice to women writers from Jamaica, Taiwan, Mauritius, Venezuela, Pakistan, Iran, and industrialized countries such as France and Australia. The editors provide each piece of prose and poetry with a "'social context' that illustrates both the possibility and extent to which these words can gain exposure in their respective societies."

SUPPLEMENTARY LIST OF PAMPHLETS AND ARTICLES

TIIIRD WORLD

Adamson, Leslie. *More to Lose Than Their Chains.* Available from Women's International Resource Exchange. *New Internationalist,* 89. 65 cents.

Bunch, Charlotte, and Shirley Castley, eds. *Developing Strategies for the Future: Feminist Perspectives.* Available from International Women's Tribune Centre (New York). 1980. 44pp. $4.

Celebrating Women World-wide. Off Our Backs 16, no. 3 (March 1986). 40pp. $1.

Economic Justice for Women. United Methodist Church, Board of Church and Society. *engage/social action* 100 (Jan. 1984). 31pp. 50 cents. Ellwood, Wayne. *Sisterhood's Success.* Available from Women's International Resource Exchange. *New Internationalist,* no. 90.

Elson, Diane, and Ruth Pearson. *Subordination of Women and the Internationalization of Factory Production.* Women's International Resource Exchange. 1981. 12pp. $1.40.

Flora, Cornelia B., and Richard P. Haynes. *Women and Agriculture.* University of Florida, Dept. of Philosophy. *Agriculture and Human Values* 2, no. 1 (1985).

International Sisterhood: Poetry, Fiction, and News from across the World. Spare Rib, no. 152 (March 1985). 70pp. $1.50.

Lovel, Hermione, and Marie-Therese Feuerstein. *Women, Poverty, and Community Development.* Oxford University Press. *Community Development Journal: An International Forum* 20, no. 2 (July 1985). $14.

Lycette, Margaret A., and Cecilia Jaramillo. *Low-Income Housing: A Women's Perspective.* International Center for Research on Women. April 1984. 54pp. $5.

Short Circuit: Women on the Global Assembly Line. Participatory Research Group. Sept. 1985. 39pp.

Summary of INSTRAW Series of Studies on the Role of Women in International Economic Relations. UN International Research and Training Institute for the Advancement of Women. *Policy Paper,* no. 1, June 1985. 80pp.

Urbieta, Itziar Lozano. *Women, the Key to Liberation.* Catholic Committee on Urban Ministry/Women's International Resource Exchange. *Women in Dialogue.* 1979. 8pp. 70 cents.

Women Creating a New World. Oxfam America. *Facts for Action,* no. 3. n.d. 6pp. 25 cents.

Women Workers in Multinational Enterprises in Developing Countries. UN Centre on TNCs and the Bureau of Multinational Enterprises, ILO. 1985. 119pp.

Women and Multinationals. Women's International Resource Exchange. *Multinational Monitor.* 23pp. $1.50.

Women and Production. Non-Formal Education Information Center, Michigan State University, College of Education. *NFE Exchange,* no. 22, 1981. 28pp. $2.

Women for Peace. Isis International. *Isis Women's International Bulletin,* no. 26 (1983). 40pp. $3.

Women in Development. Non-Formal Education Information Center, Michigan State University, College of Education. *NFE Exchange,* no. 13, 1978. 20pp. $2.

Women's World. Isis International. *Isis Women's International Bulletin,* no. 29, 1983. 40pp. $3.

Women: The Issue. Immaculate Heart College Center. *Global Pages* 3, no. 1, Jan./Feb. 1985. 8pp. 25 cents.

AFRICA

Due, Jean M. *How Do Rural Women Perceive Development? A Case Study in Zambia.* Women in International Development, Michigan State University. *Working Papers on Women in International Development,* no. 63, 1984. 19pp. $2.50.

Jules-Rosette, Bennetta. *Women's Work in the Informal Sector: A Zambian Case Study.* Women in International Development, Michigan State University. *Working Papers on Women in International Development,* no. 3, 1982. 24pp. $2.75.

Staudt, Kathleen. *Women's Politics and Capitalist Transformation in Subsaharan Africa.* Women in International Development, Michigan State University. *Working Papers on Women in International Development,* no. 54, 1984. 29pp. $2.75.

ASIA AND PACIFIC

Armstrong, M. Jocelyn. *Women's Friendships in the Context of Adaptation to Urban Living: A Malaysian Study.* Women in International Development, Michigan State University. *Working Papers on Women in International Development,* no. 70, 1984. 16pp. $2.50.

McLellan, Susan. *Reciprocity or Exploitation? Mothers and Daughters in the Changing Economy of Rural Malaysia.* Women in International Development, Michigan State University. *Working Papers on Women in International Development,* no. 93, 1985. 19pp. $2.50.

Miller, Barbara D. *Son Preference, Daughter Neglect, and Juvenile Sex Ratios: Pakistan and Bangladesh Compared.* Women in International Development, Michigan State University. *Working Papers on Women in International Development,* no. 30, 1983. 20pp. $2.50.

Potter, Sulamith Heins. *Birth Planning in Rural China: A Cultural Account.* Women in International Development, Michigan State University. *Working Papers on Women in International Development,* no. 103, 1985. 25pp. $2.75.

Sambamoorthi, Usha. *Labor Market Discrimination against Women in India.* Women in International Development, Michigan State University. *Working Papers on Women in International Development,* no. 58, 1984. 16pp. $2.50.

Tiffany, Sharon W. *Paradigms of Power: Feminist Reflections on the Anthropology of Women in Pacific Island Societies.* Women in International Development, Michigan State University. *Working Papers on Women in International Development,* no. 79, 1985. 35pp. $3.

Tse, Christina. *Invisible Control: Management Control of Workers in a U.S. Electronics Company.* Centre for the Progress of Peoples. 1981. 70pp. $2.50.

Women in Asia. Asia Society. *Focus on Asian Studies* 3, no. 3 (Spring 1984). 62pp. $2.

Wong, Aline K., and Yiu-Chung Ko. *Women's Work and Family Life: The Case of Electronics Workers in Singapore.* Women in International Development, Michigan State University. *Working Papers on Women in International Development,* no. 64, 1984. 37pp. $3.

LATIN AMERICA AND CARIBBEAN

AMNLAE. *Wherever a Woman Is, She Should Make Revolution.* Latin American Working Group. 1985. $3.

Association of Salvadoran Women. *Participation of Latin American Women in Social and Political Organizations: Reflections of Salva-*

doran Women. Women's International Resource Exchange. *Monthly Review,* June 1982. 7pp. 90 cents.

Babb, Florence E. *Economic Crisis and the Assault on Marketers in Peru.* Women in International Development, Michigan State University. *Working Papers on Women in International Development,* no. 6, 1982. 16pp. $2.50.

Biles, Robert E. *Women and Political Participation in Latin America: Urban Uruguay and Colombia.* Women in International Development, Michigan State University. *Working Papers on Women in International Development,* no. 25, 1983. 23pp. $2.75.

Canino, Glorisa J., Milagros Bravo-Corrada, and Maritza Rubio-Stipec. *The Role of Women in Puerto Rican Television.* Women in International Development, Michigan State University. *Working Papers on Women in International Development,* no. 99, 1985. 13pp. $2.25.

Casal, Lourdes. *Revolution and "Conciencia": Women in Cuba.* Women's International Resource Exchange. 1980. 12pp. $1.35.

Crummett, María de los Ángeles. *Class, Household Structure, and Migration: A Case Study from Rural Mexico.* Women in International Development, Michigan State University. *Working Papers on Women in International Development,* no. 92, 1985. 31pp. $3.

Deere, Carmen Diana. *Rural Women and State Policy: The Latin American Agrarian Reform Experience.* Women in International Development, Michigan State University. *Working Papers on Women in International Development,* no. 81, 1985. 32pp. $3.

Guatemala: The Compañeras Speak. Guatemala News and Information Bureau. 24pp. 50 cents.

Harman, Inge Maria. *Women and Cooperative Labor in the Southern Bolivian Andes.* Women in International Development, Michigan State University. *Working Papers on Women in International Development,* no. 65, 1984. 10pp. $2.25.

Ireson, Carol J. *Development, Women's Situation, and Fertility: The Mexican Case.* Women in International Development, Michigan State University. *Working Papers on Women in International Development,* no. 95, 1985. 30pp. $3.

Rosenberg, Terry Jean. *Women's Productive and Reproductive Roles in the Family Wage Economy: A Colombian Example.* Women in International Development, Michigan State University. *Working Papers on Women in International Development,* no. 68, 1984. 26pp. $2.75.

Rupert, Linda Marguerite, with research assistance from Ana Maria Hakim. *Women in Peru: Voices from a Decade.* ECO–Andes. 1986. 54pp. $6, postage included.

Update: The Case of Four U.S. Churchwomen Murdered in El Salvador in December 1980. Lawyers Committee for International Human Rights. May 1984. 31pp. $4.

Women and War in El Salvador. Women's International Resource Exchange. 1982. 44pp. $2.50.

MIDDLE EAST

Dearden, Ann, ed. *Arab Women.* Minority Rights Group. *MRG Report,* no. 27, 1983. 16pp. $4.

Exodus to Middle East. Centre for Society and Religion. November 1985. 63pp.

INFORMATION SOURCES

Periodicals from women's organizations such as International Women's Tribune Centre (*Tribune*), Isis International (*Women's Journal*) and Peoples Translation Service (*Connexions*) are often devoted to one theme. As such they make excellent resources for group or individual study. Write to the publishers for a catalog of their back issues.

Other organizations, such as the Women and Development Programme of the Institute of Social Studies and the Women in International Development office at Michigan State University, maintain backlists of their working papers and studies.

The Women's International Resource Exchange publishes a regular catalog of pamphlets and articles that are available directly from WIRE.

See also these publications from **Third World Resources**, 464 19 St., Oakland, CA 94612:

Asia and Pacific: A Directory of Resources. Compiled and edited by Thomas P. Fenton and Mary J. Heffron. Maryknoll, N.Y., and London: Orbis Books and Zed Books, 1986. 160pp. $9.95, plus $1.50 shipping and handling. Illustrations and indexes.

Latin America and Caribbean: A Directory of Resources. Compiled and edited by Thomas P. Fenton and Mary J. Heffron. Maryknoll, N.Y., and London: Orbis Books and Zed Books, 1986. 160pp. $9.95, plus $1.50 shipping and handling. Illustrations and indexes.

Resource directories on Africa and on the Middle East are forthcoming from Orbis and Zed in 1987.

Third World Resource Directory: A Guide to Organizations and Publications. Edited by Thomas P. Fenton and Mary J. Heffron. Maryknoll, N.Y.: Orbis Books, 1984. 304pp. $17.95, plus $1.50 shipping and handling. Illustrations, indexes.

The pamphlets and articles section (pp. 230–35) of the chapter on women should be consulted, along with the listings of pamphlets and articles in the other nine chapters.

Third World Resources: A Quarterly Review of Resources from and about the Third World. 4 issues/year. Newsletter. 28cm. 16pp. $25/year (organizational subscription), $25/two years (individual subscription). Inquire for overseas rates. Subscriptions are available on a calendar-year basis only.

See also the bibliographies, catalogs, and directories in the books chapter above for lists of other booklets related to women in the Third World.

5

Audiovisuals

This chapter is divided into two parts: visual resources (films, filmstrips, slideshows, and videotapes) and audio resources (records and tapes). Each part is divided into three sections: annotated entries, supplementary list, and sources of additional information.

It was impossible for us to preview all the audiovisuals included in this directory. In the case of resources that we were unable to evaluate personally, we have quoted directly from the distributor's description of the audiovisual or from annotations in other directories. The source is given in small capital letters at the end of each annotation: DIST = distributor; AFCA = *Access to Films on Central America* (see p. 117 below).

We have done our best to select audiovisuals that appear to be worthy of your consideration, but we caution you to arrange for previews of audiovisuals to determine their appropriateness in your setting.

All audiovisuals are integrated into the titles index at the back of this directory. See the organizations index for the addresses of distributors listed in this chapter.

(See p. 119 for the introduction to the audio resources section.)

VISUAL RESOURCES

Information in the **annotated entries** is given in the following order: title; producer(s); director(s); date; length (in minutes); format; principal rental and purchase price; secondary distributor(s); description of content; and source of annotation.

When an audiovisual is available from distributors other than the principal one, we have listed those as secondary distributors, but in deference to the rights of the principal distributor we have omitted the often lower rental rates of the secondary distributors. You are free, of course, to make your own inquiries. Rental/purchase information should be taken only as being indicative. We urge you to inquire about all fees and conditions before ordering an audiovisual. Some distributors have sliding price scales depending upon the nature of your organization and the intended use of the audiovisual, so it is advisable to ask about discounts when you make your inquiry.

Visual resources in the **supplementary list** (pp. 113–116) are grouped under these headings: Third World; Africa; Asia and Pacific; and Latin America and Caribbean.

The **information sources** section (pp. 116–119) provides information on guides and catalogs that contain the names of other visual resources related to women in the Third World.

ANNOTATED ENTRIES

And That is Why the State is to Blame. **Produced by Stichting Derde Cinema. Directed by Frank Diamand and Jan van der Putten. 1984. Color film and videocassette. Distributed by New Time Films. Rental: $85. Purchase: $850 (film), $575 (video).**

"And That is Why the State is to Blame is a film about Marianella Garcia Villas, president of the Human Rights Commission of El Salvador, who was killed by the Salvadoran army on March 14, 1983. She had returned in secret to conduct an investigation into the use of chemical weapons and indiscriminate bombing of the civilian population.

"The film describes Marianella's heroic and unceasing fight against injustice and brutality in her country. Through interviews with her family, friends and colleagues, the film reveals a portrait of an untiring and dedicated woman; a lawyer from an affluent family, she was one of the very few willing to defend political prisoners.

"Marianella cleaned up and photographed hundreds of bodies found lying in the streets so that families could identify them. She travelled around the world with photographs, documents and statements of witnesses testifying to the violations of human rights in El Salvador. She is seen in various countries pleading for international support. Her taped diary covering the last weeks of her life, the interviews with eyewitnesses, and the photographs she took, show the horrors of war and the undeniable bombardment of the civilian population. Two Salvadoran witnesses smuggled out of the country and the American doctor Charles Clements—who worked in a liberated area from March 1982 to March 1983—describe bombardments with napalm and white phosphorus.

"And That is Why the State is to Blame is a double portrait of the state of human rights in El Salvador and of the woman who sacrificed her life in defense of those rights." DIST

Asante Market Women. **Produced by Granada Television International. 1983. 52 minutes. Videocassette. Distributed by Filmakers Library. Rental: $75. Purchase: $445.**

"In the Asante tribe of Ghana, men are polygamous and women are subordinate in all domestic matters. But surprisingly, there is one arena where women reign supreme—the market place. These tough, assertive women have evolved their own power structure. A head woman — the Queenmother — arbitrates all disputes over price and quality. Amidst the noise and color of the Kumasi Central Market we perceive the intricacies of this matrilineal society." DIST

Basta Ya! Women in Central America. **Produced by the Resource Center. 1983. 25 minutes. Color slideshow with cassette tape. Distributed by the Resource Center. Rental: $25 per week. Purchase: $65 (individuals or groups), $100 (businesses or institutions). Also available from Women's International Resource Exchange.**

"*Basta Ya!* portrays the daily life of rural and urban Central American women. The show also looks at the role of the U.S. government and corporations in these women's lives, as well as the traumatic effects of war." DIST

Chile: Four Women's Stories. **Produced by the American Friends Service Committee. 1981. 25 minutes. Color slideshow with cassette tape, script, background materials, and action guide. Distributed by American Friends Service Committee (Cambridge). Rental: $10/15.**

"Four women speak in their own words about their lives in Chile before and after the September 11, 1973, military coup. The women are of diverse economic backgrounds. Their stories touch on Chile's history, economic conditions, the worker movement under Allende, the Chilean women's movement, repression after the coup, and commitment to the new Chilean revolution.

"Isolina, a nutritionist, belongs to an organization of women (and some men) who are relatives of people who have disappeared under the Pinochet dictatorship.

"Olga, a 70-year-old retired university professor, helped found the Chile Women's Movement in 1935.

"Manuella, born in Chile's rural south, is a widow with two sons. She has worked on committees for the development of women workers and unemployed workers.

"Maria Elena is studying to be a teacher. Her commitment takes her to the slums of Santiago to work with young people." DIST

The Compañeras Speak. **Produced by Guatemala News and Information Bureau. 1983. 24 minutes. Color slideshow with cassette tape. Distributed by Guatemala News and Information Bureau. Rental: inquire.**

"Presents testimonies of Guatemalan women involved in the liberation struggle. Background information on the situation in Guatemala is followed by the testimonies of six women from varied ethnic and class backgrounds. The women discuss their political evolution and the challenges they face as women in struggle. Depicts women's growing participation in bringing change to Guatemala." AFCA

For a Woman in El Salvador Speaking. **Produced by Sara Halprin. 1985. 7 minutes. Color film and videocassette. Distributed by Women Make Movies. Rental: $25. Purchase: $150 (film), $75 (video).**

This highly acclaimed film illustrates how Salvadoran and North

American women can collaborate artistically, politically, and financially to voice their concerns about the abuse of women and children in El Salvador and about the role of women in addressing those abuses.

Making powerful use of three languages (sign, Spanish, and English) and a variety of cultural forms (murals, poetry, music), *For a Woman* dramatizes the story of Claudina Calderón, a twenty-nine-year-old pregnant student at the University of El Salvador who was abducted with her infant son and three other women and their children by government security forces in 1983.

The film was produced in cooperation with the Women's Association of El Salvador (AMES) and Friends of AMES, a sister organization with chapters in the United States and Canada.

For the Children of El Salvador. **Produced by AMES (Women's Association of El Salvador). 1984. 20 minutes. Color slideshow with script or music-only cassette tape. Distributed by AMES. Rental: inquire.**

"Describes the political and economic situation in El Salvador and the effects of U.S. intervention, focusing on the problems faced by women and children. Details the programs of AMES, both inside and outside of El Salvador, to promote social justice and address the many needs of women and children." AFCA

Forget Not Our Sisters. **Produced by American Friends Service Committee. 1982. 39 minutes. Color slideshow with cassette tape. Distributed by American Friends Service Committee (Cambridge). Rental: $10/15.**

"A moving and beautiful tribute to the courage of South African women, co-narrated by Barbara Brown and a black South African woman. Good overview of apartheid." DIST

Home Life. **Produced and directed by Julia Lesage. 1985. 27 minutes. Color videocassette. Purchase of ½-inch videocassette (VHS or Betamax) from Julia Lesage (2620 N. Richmond, Chicago, IL 60647. Tel: [312] 252–6616): $39.95 (individuals), $59.95 (institutions). Tape includes *Las Nicas* (see below). Rental or purchase of ¾-inch U-Matic videocassette from Video Data Bank. Rental: $50 (one week). Purchase: $125.**

"*Home Life* depicts the experiences of one Nicaraguan family in a way that provides an analogy to other underprivileged and peasant families in Latin America as well as elsewhere in the Third World. The guest in the home, a U.S. minister, gains an education merely by living with and knowing this family. While the dominant press might portray the minister's 'civilizing mission,' in this video we see the reverse taking place. The repositor of Christian charity and endurance is a sturdy grandmother, full of humanity in a poor environment.

"The tape lets the family relay the processes of their daily life, and it is affecting in its simplicity without ceremonizing or enervating the events or the people shown. A question constantly comes to the viewer's mind: Why such inhumane treatment? Why is anyone trying so hard to harm this family, these people of Nicaragua?

"Home Life was shot in August 1984 in Estelí, Nicaragua, a city whose people acutely feel the impact of U.S. supported contra raids. Videomakers Julia Lesage and Chuck Kleinhans and Seattle-based minister Randall Mullins lived with the people of Estelí for five weeks, and Randall made this tape with the Diaz family to introduce to his parish back home the Nicaraguan family whose life and love he shared." DIST

In Our Own Hands. **Produced by Third World Women. 1984. 22 minutes. Videocassette. Distributed by Third World Women's Project, Institute for Policy Studies. Rental: $30 (university), $20 (community or church). Purchase: $75. Inquire for rates for ¾-inch tape format.**

This Third World Women's Project video is an interview with Magda Enríquez, a founder of AMNLAE, the Nicaraguan women's association. In early 1984 Ms. Enríquez traveled to fifteen cities in the United States and England to discuss the advances Nicaraguan women have made since the 1979 revolution, U.S. policy in Nicaragua, and Nicaraguan democracy.

Maids and Madams. **Produced by Mira Hamermesh. 1985. 60 minutes. Videocassette. Distributed by Filmakers Library. Rental: $75. Purchase: $445.**

"In South Africa many white children are brought up by black South African women who transfer to them the love they would otherwise have devoted to their own children.

"'Some madams are kind, some ruthlessly exploit their black maids, but the tragedy of the black woman is that in order to survive she has to look after her madam's children and neglect her own,' says an enlightened madam.

"Over a million black women live in a state of domestic bondage, underpaid, working long hours and at the mercy of draconian laws, which separate them from their own families. Apartheid, like charity, begins at home and madam's bedroom, kitchen and nursery are the open battle zones where the desperate struggle for racial and sexual domination takes place.

"Mira Hamermesh's understated yet powerful film, shot recently in South Africa, eloquently examines the issues of apartheid through this particular emotional relationship — black maid and white madam — which may well determine the outcome of racial confrontation in that country." DIST

Las Nicas. **Produced and directed by Julia Lesage. 1985. 45 minutes. Color videocassette. Purchase of ½-inch videocassette (VHS or Betamax) from Julia Lesage (2620 N. Richmond, Chicago, IL 60647. Tel: [312] 252-6616): $39.95 (individuals), $59.95 (institutions). Tape includes *Home Life* (see above). Rental or purchase of ¾-inch U-Matic videocassette from Video Data Bank. Rental: $75 (one week). Purchase: $125.**

"In 1981 and 1982, Carole Issacs and Julia Lesage visited Nicaragua and did in-depth interviews with women in the Managua area. Here Nicaraguan women speak about the topics of work, sexual politics, religion, family life, children, social participation, and defense.

"*Las Nicas* is about how women survive in the face of overwhelming force and pressures. The tape shows a discernible link between the country's survival and women's total emancipation. 'This is a women's revolution,' intones one woman as she vows to defend it at any cost. These women's obduracy accentuates the underlying strength of their commitment. Somoza's Nicaragua is littered with the blood and bones of innocent women and their children. The work offers an excellent tribute to the fallen and to the living who are determined not to have history repeat itself." DIST

La Operación. **Directed by Ana María García. 1982. 40 minutes. Color film and videocassette. Distributed by Cinema Guild. Rental: $65. Purchase: $595 (film), $395 (tape).**

"Puerto Rico is the country with the highest incidence of female sterilization in the world. Over one-third of all Puerto Rican women of childbearing age have been sterilized. So common is the operation that it is simply known as *la operación*.

"Using newsreels and excerpts from government propaganda films plus interviews with Puerto Rican women, doctors, birth control specialists, politicians and others, this powerful documentary explores the controversial use of sterilization as a means of population control." DIST

Overview: Development and Women. **Produced by United Nations Development Programme. 1980. 15 minutes. Color slideshow with script and discussion guide. Distributed by Mennonite Central Committee (Akron office only). Rental: free.**

"Explores development planners' traditional attitudes toward women, their effects and the essential new directions development must take." DIST

Perhaps Women Are More Economical. **Produced and directed by Saskia Wieringa and Elsje Plantema. 1983. 27 minutes. Color film. Distributed by the Institute of Social Studies, Women and Development Programme. Purchase: inquire.**

"The majority of Javanese women perform multiple occupations: most of them find employment in agriculture and many of these combine their work in the fields with labour in [home] industries. As is the case with many poor women in the cities of Central Java, the batik industry is one of their main employers. Transformations in agriculture and in the batik industries threaten the employment of many thousands of Javanese women. The present military government pays no attention to the rising levels of unemployment, the extremely low wages, and the bad labour conditions of the women batik workers. Their argument is that the 'women are married anyway and only earn a little on the side.'

"This film shows the development of the batik industry from its origins at the courts of the Central Javanese princes to the workshops and factories of today. The producers of traditional batik—and here mainly women are employed—are faced with growing competition for declining markets. The 'modern' batik, which is being made mainly for export and for the tourist market, is the only type of batik with a growing market. This batik is mainly made by men who are suddenly called not batik workers, as the women workers are, but batik 'artists.' Their wages are many times higher than those of their female colleagues. The only answer we received when we asked why this was so is: "Women have fewer needs. Maybe women are more economical . . .'" DIST

The Price of Change. **Produced by Elizabeth Fernea. Directed by Marilyn Gaunt. 1982. 26 minutes. Color film and videocassette with teacher's study guide. Distributed by Icarus Films. Rental: $50 (film only). Purchase: $425 (film), $260 (video).**

"For sixty years Egyptian women have been gradually entering all sectors of the public work force. Work outside the home, once considered shameful, has today become a necessity. Today, nearly forty percent of Egyptian women contribute in some way to providing the family income.

"*The Price of Change* examines the consequences of work for five women — a factory worker with four children, a rural village leader involved in family planning, a doctor, a social worker, and a member of Parliament who is also speaker for the opposition party.

"The film presents a picture of changing attitudes to work, the family, sex, and women's place in society." DIST

Refugee Women. **Produced by United Nations High Commission for Refugees. 1980. 32 minutes. Color slideshow with script. Distributed by Mennonite Central Committee (Akron office only). Rental: free.**

"The majority of refugees in the world today are women and girls. It is especially traumatic for them to be uprooted from their homes. This informative slide set, with study guides and background papers, helps us to gain a better understanding of the special problems of refugee women. It indicates some of their needs and why it is necessary to help them." DIST

Roses in December. **Produced by Ana Carrigan and Bernard Stone. 1982. 56 minutes. Color film and videocassette. Distributed by First Run Films. Rental: $100. Purchase: $850 (film), $500 (video). Also from American Friends Service Committee (Cambridge).**

"On December 2, 1980, lay missioner Jean Donovan and three North American nuns were brutally murdered by the government security forces in El Salvador. Narrated by John Houseman, *Roses in December* chronicles the brief life of Jean Donovan with sensitivity and compassion, revealing her growing commitment to the poor during a period of the Salvadoran government's most violent repression.

"Award-winning filmmakers Ana Carrigan and Bernard Stone have skillfully woven the story of the personal tragedy of the deaths of Jean and Sisters Dorothy Kazel, Ita Ford and Maura Clark, with the complex political issues of American military support and involvement with the military leaders of El Salvador.

"*Roses in December* is more than an eloquent memorial to a courageous woman. While tracing the steps that led this young, conservative woman to become a lay missioner in the middle of a war zone, the film provides a thought-provoking comment on U.S. foreign policy in Central America." DIST

Small Happiness: Women of a Chinese Village. **Produced by Carma Hinton and Richard Gordon, with Kathy Kline and Dan Sipe. 1985. 58 minutes. Color film and videocassette. Distributed by New Day Films. Rental: $90. Purchase: $800 (film), $480 (video).**

"In rural China a newborn son is called 'great happiness,' but a newborn daughter is often a 'small happiness.' *Small Happiness* is a powerful exploration of sexual politics. Chinese women speak frankly about footbinding, the new birth control policy, work, love, and marriage." DIST

South Africa Belongs to Us: The Struggle of the Black Women of South Africa. **Produced by Chris Austin, Peter Chappell, and Ruth Weiss. 1980. 57 minutes. Color film and videocassette. Distributed by Icarus Films. Rental: $65. Purchase: $575 (film), $560 (video).**

"A film on the lives of black women in South Africa, shot secretly with the help of two black women journalists. With observational portraits of five ordinary women and interviews with women activists, *South Africa Belongs to Us* depicts the struggle of the black woman for dignity in the face of apartheid: from the struggle for a roof over her head and food for her children, to black consciousness and the total liberation of her people.

"Helped by the people involved and working covertly the film makers were able to gain access for the first time to places like the huge segregated barracks built for so-called migrant workers, where women are condemned to spend their working lives separated from their families. Four thousand women live four to a room in a huge prison-like building with barred gates and a jail for 'offenders.'" DIST

South Africa Belongs to Us includes interviews with a woman in the arid countryside of the black reserves, a woman working as a maid and nanny in a white household, two members of the women's committee in a shanty town outside of Cape Town, a young leader from the outlawed Black Consciousness Movement, and with Winnie Mandela, the banned and banished women's leader who has become a symbol of resistance in South Africa.

The Two Worlds of Angelita. **Produced by Jane Morrison. 1982. 77 minutes. Color film and videocassette. In Spanish with English subtitles. Distributed by First Run Films. Rental: $150 (film only). Purchase: $1,150 (film), $700 (video).**

"*The Two Worlds of Angelita* is the story of a young Puerto Rican family who live in two cultures—their own and the American one—as they try to maintain their own identity and traditions. Their story, told through the eyes of nine-year-old Angelita, begins in a small town on the island and ends in the barrio of New York's Lower East Side. In their search for a better life on the mainland, the young family must overcome obstacles which all immigrants face: language barriers, racism, housing problems, financial difficulties and the challenge of breaking traditional bonds and coping with a new alien culture. The film sensitively conveys Angelita's reactions to these new experiences and their effect on each member of the family." DIST

A Veiled Revolution. **Produced by Elizabeth Fernea. Directed by Marilyn Gaunt. 1982. 26 minutes. Color film and videocassette, with teacher's study guide. Distributed by Icarus Films. Rental: $50 (film only). Purchase: $425 (film), $260 (video).**

"Egypt was the first Arab country where women marched in political demonstrations (1919); the first where women took off the veil (1923); and the first to offer free public secular education to women (1924). Today the granddaughters of those early Arab feminists are returning to traditional garb, sometimes with full face veil and gloves, which they call Islamic dress.

"What are the reasons for this new movement? Is it an echo of the Iranian revolution? Is it a rejection of Western values? What do women themselves say about it? *A Veiled Revolution* looks at some of this history, and attempts to answer some of these questions." DIST

When the Mountains Tremble. **Directed by Pamela Yates and Thomas Sigel. 1983. 83 minutes. Color film. Distributed by New Yorker Films. Rental: $350. Also from IDERA films.**

"*When the Mountains Tremble* is a vigorous and persuasive documentary describing the struggle of the largely Indian peasantry in Guatemala against a heritage of state and foreign (i.e., U.S.) oppression. Loosely centered on the experiences of a 23-year-old Indian woman now living in exile, the film knits a variety of forms — interview, newsreel, reenactment, video transmission, and on-the-spot footage shot at great hazard — into a wide-ranging and remarkably cohesive epic canvas of the Guatemalan struggle." DIST

Women in Development: The Neglected Key. **Produced by Mennonite Central Committee. 1981. 17 minutes. Color filmstrip with script and study guide. Distributed by Mennonite Central Committee (all offices except Great Lakes). Rental: free.**

"Explores the problems and potential of women in development. Wherever people are poor and hungry, women are the poorest and the hungriest. Yet, these women have important roles in their societies, roles that are often ignored." DIST

Women in Nicaragua: The Second Revolution. **Produced by Jackie Reiter. 1982. Color film and videocassette. Distributed by Icarus Films. Rental: $55 (film only). Purchase: $495 (film), $280 (video). Also from IDERA Films and Women Make Movies.**

"This documentary explores the efforts of women to gain equality and to combat machismo as part of Nicaragua's 'second revolution.'

"The film features scenes with Gladys Baez, the first woman to join the Sandinista guerrilla forces in the early 1960s. She is also seen talking with women soldiers about the problems they face, including chauvinism, lack of respect, and a double work day.

"*Women in Nicaragua* also looks at women's contribution to the Nicaraguan economy and it explores different steps which the Sandinista government, and women themselves, are taking to integrate women more fully into all aspects of society." DIST

Women of the Planet (Mujeres del Planeta). **Produced by María Barea. 1984. 28 minutes. Color film and videocassette. Distributed by Women Makes Movies. Rental: $60. Purchase: $250 (video only).**

"Winner of the Silver Dove at the Leipzig Film Festival, this film shows the dignity of women in a shantytown outside Lima, Peru as they organize for better living conditions." DIST

Women under Apartheid. **1980. Photo exhibit. 14 sheets. 67 photographs and text. Distributed by International Defense and Aid Fund for Southern Africa. Purchase: $12.75, plus postage.**

"Shows how apartheid policies—e.g., migrant labor system, resettlement programs and influx control—have especially affected the lives of women. Depicts the role of women in the liberation struggle." DIST

Women under Siege. **Produced by Elizabeth Fernea. Directed by Marilyn Gaunt. 1982. 26 minutes. Color film and videocassette. Distributed by Icarus Films. Rental: $50 (film only). Purchase: $425 (film), $260 (video).**

"Rashadiyah is a town six miles north of the Israeli border, in southern Lebanon. Once a peaceful agricultural village, in 1964 it became the setting for a camp housing 14,000 Palestinian refugees. For years they lived under constant harassment and threat of Israeli attack.

"Women play a crucial role in the Palestinian community, as mothers, teachers, political organizers, farm laborers, and fighters. Through actual footage and interviews with the women of Rashadiyah, this film explores the lives of six representative Palestinian women.

"In June 1982 the town of Rashadiyah was bombed and attacked by Israeli forces. The camp was reduced to ruins, many of the residents forced to flee." DIST

You Have Struck a Rock. **Produced by Deborah May. 1981. 28 minutes. Color film. Distributed by California Newsreel. Rental: $50. Purchase: $450.**

"Women took the lead in mobilizing mass opposition to apartheid during the 1950s when the South African regime attempted to extend the hated pass system to them. 'You have touched a woman, you have struck a rock' became the slogan of the anti-pass campaigns.

"Utilizing techniques of civil disobedience familiar from the Civil Rights Movement [in the United States], women refused to accept their passes or gathered and burnt them publicly. The government responded with increased violence, new laws, and imprisonment. It was only after a decade of resistance culminating with the Sharpeville Massacre, the banning of political organizations and the imprisonment of the leaders, that the regime finally succeeded in imposing the passes.

"Lillian Ngoyi, Helen Joseph, Dora Tamana, Frances Baard, and others tell their stories, illustrated with archival footage, punctuated by South African music. Their lives, and this film, are a tribute to the spirit and perseverance of Black South African women." DIST

SUPPLEMENTARY LIST OF VISUAL RESOURCES

THIRD WORLD

A Zenana: Scenes and Recollections. Color film. Distributor: Documentary Educational Resources, 5 Bridge St., Watertown, MA 02172. Rental: $45. Purchase: $500.

As Strong as the Land. Color filmstrip with script. Distributor: United Methodist Church, Women's Division.

I Have Three Children of My Own. Produced by Packard Manse Media Project. 1979. Color slideshow with script. Distributor: Packard Manse Media Project.

The Issue Is Women. 1982. Color slideshow with cassette tape. Distributor: International Women's Tribune Centre.

Small Interventions: The Role of Women in Development. Distributor: Oxfam America. Rental: $15.

Women in Production. Color slideshow with script. Distributor: Development Education Media Service.

Women in World Cultures. Produced by Marjorie Wall Bingham and Susan Hill Gross. Multimedia program. Distributor: Gem Publications, 411 Mallalieu Dr., Hudson, WI 54016.

Women of the World. 1975. Color film. Distributor: ROA Films.

Women of the World Meet Together. Color slideshow with cassette tape. Distributor: International Women's Tribune Centre.

Women on the Global Assembly Line. Directed by Lorraine Gray. Color film. Distributor: Educational TV and Film Center.

World Feminists. Color film and videocassette. Distributor: Martha Stuart Communications.

AFRICA

Awake from Mourning. Produced by Betty Wolpert. 1981. Color film and videocassette. Distributor: Villon Films.

Crossroads/South Africa. Produced by Jonathan Wacks. 1980. Color film and videocassette. Distributor: California Newsreel.

Life and Work of Nomadic Women in Somalia. Produced by Amina Warsame. 1985. Color slideshow with cassette tape. 70 slides. Distributor: Institute of Social Studies, Women and Development Programme. Purchase: inquire.

Re'assemblage. Directed by Trinh T. Minh-ha. 1983. Color film. Distributor: Circles.

Souls in the Sun. 1982. Color film. Distributor: Extension Media Center, University of California—Berkeley. Rental: $33. Made for the United Nations.

South Africa. Color film and videocassette. Distributor: Concord Films Council.

We Carry a Heavy Load. Color slideshow with script. Distributor: Zimbabwe Women's Bureau.

Working for a Change. Directed by Wien De Smit. 1985. Color slideshow with script. Distributor: Zimbabwe Women's Bureau.

ASIA AND PACIFIC

After the Difficulties: Working Women in Southeast Asia. Produced by Souad Sharabani and Helene Klodawsky. 1982. Color slideshow with script. Distributor: Development Education Centre (Toronto).

Another Beginning. 1984. Color film. In Korean with English subtitles. Distributor: Korean Women's Development Institute.

Can You Hear Us. 1984. Videocassette. Distributor: Asian Christian Forum on Development.

Chinese Women: Now We Hold Up Half the Sky. Produced by Nancy Henningsen. Color slideshow with cassette tape. 70 slides and research kit. Distributor: U.S.-China People's Friendship Association.

Dadi and Her Family. Color film. Distributor: Film Distribution Office, Dept. of South Asian Studies, University of Wisconsin—Madison. Rental: $30. Purchase: $295.

East Sepik Women's Network. Color slideshow with script. Distributor: Gavien Women's Development Group.

From Nothing to Something. Produced by Christian Industrial Committee. Color slideshow with script. Distributor: Christian Industrial Committee.

Gui Dao—On the Way, Some Chinese Women Told Us . . . Color film and videocassette. 3 parts. Distributor: National Film Board of Canada. Rental: $90. Purchase: $875 (film), $500 (video).

India's Working Women. Produced by Geraldine Forbes. Color filmstrip with cassette tape. Includes teacher's guide. Distributor: Education Resources Center, State Education Dept., Rm. 9B52, Albany, NY 12230. Purchase: $20.

Korea: Families of the World. Produced by Journal Films. Color film. Distributor: EcuFilm.

Letter from Bataan. Color slideshow with script. Distributor: Center for Women's Resources.

Matriliny and Declining Women's Power in Minangkabau, Indonesia. Produced by Saskia Wieringa. 1985. Color slideshow with cassette tape. 80 slides. Distributor: Institute of Social Studies, Women and Development Programme. Purchase: inquire.

Munni ("Little Girl"): Childhood and Art in Mithila. Color film. Distributor: Film Distribution Office, Dept. of South Asian Studies, University of Wisconsin – Madison. Rental: $25. Purchase: $250.

Olongapo. 1981. Color slideshow with script. Distributor: Asian Social Institute.

The Other Half of the Sky: A China Memoir. Produced by Claudia Weill and Shirley MacLaine. Color film. Distributor: New Day Films.

Pakistani Women. Directed by Linda Mather. Color slideshow with script. Available from Linda Mather, Dept. of Higher Education, 225 W. State St., CN 542, Trenton, NJ 08625.

Power to the Women in Us. Color slideshow with script. Distributor: Center for Women's Resources.

Seirl. Produced by Christian Industrial Committee. Color film. Distributor: Christian Industrial Committee.

Small Intervention: The Role of Women in India's Development. Color slideshow with script. Distributor: Oxfam–America.

Story of Ah Jen. Color slideshow with script. Distributor: Christian Industrial Committee.

Stree Mukti Yatra (Journey for Women's Liberation). Produced by Chhaya Datar. 1985. Color slideshow with cassette tape. 42 slides. Distributor: Institute of Social Studies, Women and Development Programme. Purchase: inquire.

Three Generations of Javanese Women. Directed by Martha Stuart. Videocassette. Distributor: Martha Stuart Communications.

We Thai Women. Directed by Siriporn Skrobanek. Color slideshow with script. Thai and English. Distributor: Women's Information Center.

Women Activists in Asia. Color slideshow with script. Distributor: YWCA Audio-Visual Materials Resource Center.

Women in Asian Development. Color slideshow with script. Distributor: YWCA Audio-Visual Materials Resource Center.

Women in China. Produced by Betty McAfee. Color film and videocassette. Distributor: Educational Development Center, 55 Chapel St., Newton, MA 02160. Rental: $40 (film only). Purchase: $405 (film), $325 (video).

Women in Development. Color slideshow with script. Distributor: Kahayag Foundation.
Women in Vietnam. 1973. Color slideshow with script. Distributor: American Friends Service Committee (Cambridge).

LATIN AMERICA AND CARIBBEAN

Blood of the Condor. Produced by Jorge Sanjines. 1969. Black and white film. Distributor: New Yorker Films.
The Dead Are Not Silent. Produced by Studio H & S of the German Democratic Republic. 1978. Black and white film. Distributor: New Time Films.
The Double Day. Produced by Helena Solberg-Ladd. 1975. Color film. Distributor: Cinema Guild.
Dutty Tuff: Women's Work and the 1938 Struggle in Jamaica. Produced by Joan French and Honor Ford-Smith. 1985. Color slideshow with cassette tape. 40 slides. Distributor: Institute of Social Studies, Women and Development Programme. Purchase: inquire.
Portrait of Teresa. Directed by Pastor Vega. 1979. Color film. Distributor: New Yorker Films.
Simplemente Jenny. Produced by Helena Solberg-Ladd. 1975. Color film. Distributor: Cinema Guild.
Sweet Sugar Rage. Directed by Honor Ford-Smith and Harclyde Wolcott. 1985. Color film and videocassette. In Jamaican dialect with English subtitles. Distributor: Sistren.
With the Cuban Women. Directed by Octavio Cortázar. 1975. Color film. Distributor: New Yorker Films.
Women and Work in Rosehall (St. Vincent, Caribbean). Produced by Beryl Carasco and Wendy Rodney. 1985. Color slideshow with cassette tape. 40 slides. Distributor: Institute of Social Studies, Women and Development Programme. Purchase: inquire.
Women in Arms. Produced by Victoria Schultz. 1981. Color film. Distributor: Villon Films.
Xica. Directed by Carlos Diegues. 1976. Color film. Distributor: New Yorker Films.

INFORMATION SOURCES

Isis International (Rome and Santiago) has performed an invaluable service in providing an outstanding guide to audiovisual resources by, for, and about women: *Powerful Images: A Women's Guide to Audiovisual Resources.* 1986. 210pp. Individuals: $12. Institutions: $20. Add $7 for airmail outside Europe.

The Isis guide
— brings together a wealth of audiovisual materials including videos, films, slideshows, and filmstrips produced by women from all over the world between 1975 and 1985.
— supplies a valuable key to understanding how women are challenging dominant myths and stereotypes, and how they see themselves.

— provides a forum for Third World and other women's groups to share their experiences in creating, using, and communicating through audiovisuals.

— combines practical tips for media production with ideas on how to make audiovisuals more effective for organizing, education, and enjoyment.

Powerful Images contains

— articles and interviews by and with a number of women's groups in Third World and other countries focusing on the role of audiovisuals in promoting social change.

— an annotated resource list with over six hundred multilingual audiovisuals on issues such as waging peace; apartheid and racism; women in struggle; empowering women for development; migrants and refugees; images of women; and reclaiming women's history. Each entry includes complete information for renting or purchasing the audiovisual.

— over 250 addresses of organizations, groups, and individuals that produce and/or distribute audiovisuals in Latin America, Asia, the Pacific, Africa, Europe, and North America.

— a bibliography of books, catalogs, and other printed materials in a variety of languages.

Media Network is a noteworthy clearinghouse of information on audiovisuals about social issues. The network's Information Center uses a computerized cross-referencing system to identify films, videotapes, and slideshows on more than two hundred topics, including women's rights, migrant workers, ethnic culture and history, and U.S. foreign and military policy. Media Network has produced concise directories of audiovisuals on Central America and on apartheid and the Southern African region. Media Network, 208 W. 13 St., New York, NY 10011. Tel: (212) 620–0877.

Consult the catalogs from the film distributors included in this directory and see the directories and guides described in the books chapter above for additional information on audiovisuals related to women in the Third World.

The following guides all contain visual resources on women in the Third World:

Access to Films on Central America. Edited by Wendy Tanowitz. CISPES/Northwest Regional Office, 5825 Telegraph Ave., Box 54B, Oakland, CA 94609. 1984. 20pp. $3.50. Sources, title and subject indexes.

Access to Films is an annotated list of one hundred films, slideshows, and videos that enable audiences "to see the faces and hear the voices of those who are at the muzzle end of U.S. foreign policy" in Central America. Listings are by country with complete title and subject indexes. There are multiple listings of low-cost materials.

Audio-Visual Resources for Social Change. American Friends Service

Committee, 2161 Massachusetts Ave., Cambridge, MA 02140. Tel: (617) 497-5273. 1981. Tabloid newspaper. 8pp. Free. Three supplements have been released: winter 1982–summer 1983 (2pp.), 1984–85 (8pp.), and 1986 (12pp.).

Audio-Visual Resources is an excellent guide for a number of reasons: it is an annotated list of over one hundred of the best audiovisuals available on social change; resources are classified under sixty-two headings, cross-referenced, and indexed; the catalog is kept up-to-date through periodic supplements; and—best of all—each of the audiovisuals listed in the catalog is available conveniently and inexpensively from the New England Regional Office of AFSC. Call to discuss rental procedures with AFSC's film librarian.

Educators Guide to Free Films. Compiled and edited by John C. Diffor and Elaine N. Diffor. Educators Progress Service, 214 Center St., Randolf, WI 53956. Annual.

The forty-fourth edition of this guide (1984) numbered 690 pages and included over 4,000 titles available in the United States and Canada.

Educators Guide to Free Filmstrips. Compiled and edited John C. Diffor and Elaine N. Diffor. Educators Progress Service (address above). Annual.

The thirty-sixth edition of this guide (1984) listed 438 titles in 148 pages.

Women in Films. United Nations Non-Governmental Liaison Service, UN DC2-1103, New York, NY 10017.

See also these publications from **Third World Resources,** 464 19 St., Oakland, CA 94612:

Asia and Pacific: A Directory of Resources. Compiled and edited by Thomas P. Fenton and Mary J. Heffron. Maryknoll, N.Y., and London: Orbis Books and Zed Books, 1986. 160pp. $9.95, plus $1.50 shipping and handling. Illustrations and indexes.

Latin America and Caribbean: A Directory of Resources. Compiled and edited by Thomas P. Fenton and Mary J. Heffron. Maryknoll, N.Y., and London: Orbis Books and Zed Books, 1986. 160pp. $9.95, plus $1.50 shipping and handling. Illustrations and indexes.

Resource directories on Africa and on the Middle East are forthcoming from Orbis and Zed in 1987.

Third World Resource Directory: A Guide to Organizations and Publications. Edited by Thomas P. Fenton and Mary J. Heffron. Maryknoll, N.Y.: Orbis Books, 1984. 304pp. $17.95, plus $1.50 shipping and handling. Illustrations, indexes.

The audiovisuals section (pp. 236–39) and the other resources section (pp. 240–43) of the chapter on women should be consulted, along with the listings of audiovisuals in the other nine chapters.

Third World Resources: A Quarterly Review of Resources from and about the Third World. 4 issues/year. Newsletter. 28cm. 16pp. $25/year (organizational subscription), $25/two years (individual subscription).

Inquire for overseas rates. Subscriptions are available on a calendar-year basis only.

AUDIO RESOURCES

Information in the **annotated entries** is given in the following order: title; artist(s) or producer(s); date; length (in feet for tapes); format (record or tape); distributor; ordering number; price; and description of content.

As with the visual resources the DIST code at the end of the annotation indicates that the description of the record or tape is the distributor's. Annotations that are not within quotation marks are our own.

Records and tapes in the **supplementary list** (pp. 123–124) are listed in alphabetical order.

The **information sources** section (p. 124) provides information on catalogs that contain the names of other audio resources related to women in the Third World.

ANNOTATED ENTRIES

A Arte de Mercedes Sosa. Mercedes Sosa. Two 12-inch long-playing records. Distributor: Ladyslipper. Order no.: Fontana C-7599316. $18.95.

"Mercedes Sosa is an Argentinian vocalist/song-interpreter/people's musician. She sings in Spanish but somehow communicates a message that is political even to those who don't speak that language. Her music was popular in Chile in the early 70s, but her records were banned when the military junta took power.

"This Brazilian import is an excellent compilation, representative of her best. It includes 'Gracias a la Vida.' The jacket contains lyrics in Spanish to aid in translation." DIST

Algo se quema allá afuera (Something Is Burning Out There). Estrella Artau. 12-inch long-playing record. Booklet with complete Spanish texts of songs with English translations. Distributor: Paredon Records. Order no.: 1032. $5.

"Estrella Artau sings of Puerto Rico, but also of other oppressed peoples in the Caribbean and Latin America. Some of her texts are taken from the Cuban poet Nicolas Guillen, Dominican poet Pedro Mir, Argentine poet Atahualpa Yupanqui, and Puerto Rican poet Noel Hernandez, but most of them are her own.

"Includes songs dedicated to martyred Chilean poet Victor Jara, Puerto Rican political prisoner Lolita Lebron, and a recently martyred Dominican woman, Mama Tingo." DIST

Angola: Songs of My People. Lilly Tchiumba. 12-inch long-playing record. Distributor: Monitor Records. Order no.: 767. $8.98.

Born in Luanda this gifted artist has dedicated her whole artistic career to the propagation of the folklore of her native Angola. She sings in her language, Kimbundo, about women and contract laborers, about mothers and fathers and their sick and dying children, and about the bread that they earn with their sweat—"bread," she observes, "that is not for us but that is made from our sweat."

Brazil: Songs of Protest. Zelia Barbosa. 12-inch long-playing record. English translation on jacket. Distributor: Monitor Records. Order No.: 717. $8.98.

"This album presents twelve of the most typical songs depicting the life of the Brazilian people. You will come to understand the peasant, the dweller in the 'Sertao' (Desert) of the Northeast as he sings of his sadness in having to leave the countryside to flee the drought, as he realizes his exploitation by the large landowner and as he hurls his protestations.

"The inhabitant of the 'favela' (slums) condemned to vegetate on the outskirts of society tells of his life, also, in these songs. He tells how he constantly waits for the train to take him to work and waits for the raise each month that has been promised him for a year. His wife waits for the baby to be born; the baby waits for what?

"This expression of protest by the young composers of popular music in Brazil, this outcry, expresses the desire to make a song an instrument to serve the people, to offer to the people a means of expressing themselves, of communicating: it marks a turning point in the evolution of the Brazilian song." DIST

Canto para una semilla: Homage to Violeta Parra. Inti-Illimani, Isabel Parra, and Mares Gonzáles. 1984. 12-inch long-playing record. Spanish and English texts. Also in cassette tape (without texts). Distributor: Monitor Records. Order no.: LP 821 (record), 51821 (tape). $8.95. Also from Ladyslipper.

"Isabel is the daughter of the pivotal Chilean songwriter Violeta Parra. On this 1984 release Isabel and Inti-Illimani, an exiled Chilean folk ensemble, recount Violeta's life in song and recitation. The title, literally 'Song for a Seed,' conveys the germination and growth of an idea and a consciousness which Violeta represented. The sections on this recording are chronological; her parents, childhood, adulthood and political life, her death and her epilogue." DIST

Corazón: Songs and Music Recorded in Peru. Rosalind Solomon. **12-inch long-playing record. Elaborate 12-inch x 12-inch illustrated booklet. Distributor: Folkways. Order no.: 34035. $10.98.**

"Solomon went to Peru in 1980 to photograph and record the people in Callejón de Huaylas and Callejón de Conchucos, a rugged area of the Ancash region in the Andes. The songs and sounds—children running in the plaza, a carnival street band, singing in the village church—represent a way of life that reaffirms physical struggle, calamity, and survival.

"The songs in this album are in Spanish with occasional refrains in Quechua, the indigenous language of the Andes. Solomon has taken poetic license with titles and translations." DIST

Interview with Sister Ita Ford. David Helvarg. **1980. 24 minutes. Cassette tape. Distributor: Pacifica Radio Archive. Order no.: PZ0029. $11.**

"Sister Ita Ford, a Maryknoll Sister, was found dead in El Salvador on December 4, 1980. A few days before her murder she was interviewed about her work in El Salvador, the food scarcity, the refugees, and liberation theology." DIST

Lebanon Forever. Fairuz. **12-inch long-playing record or cassette tape. Distributor: Ladyslipper. Order no.: Voix de L'Orient 310. $8.95.**

Lebanon Forever is by a Lebanese vocalist who is the best-known female singer in the Arab world, with a collection of over sixty recordings to her credit. The material on this record is in Arabic, with influences of traditional Lebanese music.

Making Ends Meet: Women in St. Vincent. **Produced by the Development Education Centre. 29:12 minutes. 1 unit. NFCB standard tape stock (Ampex 031). Stereo. Distributor: National Federation of Community Broadcasters. Order no.: Archive #6061. $12.**

"More than half the population of this eastern Caribbean island, often heads of households, often at the center of their communities, are women. Nevertheless they are denied access to effective power. Using conversations and presentations recorded around International Women's Day, the program looks at the state of women's lives and struggles." DIST

Mexico: Days of Struggle. Judith Reyes. **12-inch long-playing record. Booklet with complete Spanish and English texts. Distributor: Paredon Records. Order no.: 1012. $5.**

"Songs of the unfinished revolution written and sung in Spanish by Judith Reyes. Corridos [street ballads] of struggle and songs of the Mexican student movement." DIST

Mujer. Amparo Ochoa. **12-inch long-playing record or cassette tape. Distributor: Ladyslipper. Order no.: Discos Pueblo 1053. $8.95.**

"This Mexican import is by a musician who is considered to be the voice of the 'Nueva Canción Mexicana' [Mexican New Song], part of a political/cultural movement throughout Latin America with a strong musical expression." DIST

Murder in El Salvador. **Burton Segall. 1982. 33'. Cassette tape. Distributor: Pacifica Radio Archive. Order no.: KZ1224. $13.**
"Ita Ford was one of the four women killed in El Salvador in December 1980. Here her brother, Bill Ford, discusses the attitudes and actions of the U.S. government in its investigation of the crime. He also talks about Ita and reads from some of her letters." DIST

Para esta país: Cantos de lucha de Venezuela. **Gloria Martín. 12-inch long-playing record. Recorded in Venezuela, edited in Mexico. Distributor: Ladyslipper. Order no.: Nueva Cultura Latinoamericana 009.**
"*Songs of Struggle* contains Gloria Martín's original political songs, which she sings with a rich and vibrant voice. Instrumentation is lovely. The jacket contains the lyrics in Spanish." DIST

Poppie Nongena. **12-inch long-playing record or cassette tape. Distributor: Ladyslipper. Order no.: Hannibal 6301. $8.95.**
"This original cast recording of the award-winning South African play follows the life of Poppie, as she and her family endure the brutal racism of apartheid. Songs include many South African traditionals, including the unofficial Black South African anthem of struggle adopted by the African National Congress." DIST

Un río de sangre. **Violeta Parra. 12-inch long-playing record. Distributor: Ladyslipper. Order no.: Farn 91011. $8.95.**
"'A River of Blood' is a song written in lament of the deaths of five Latin American political heroes. Violeta Parra's songs are political, mourning injustice and conveying deep love for her people. Her children, Isabel and Angel, join their voices on two songs to complete the record the way Violeta Parra had conceived it." DIST

The Struggle. **Sheila Chandra. 12-inch long-playing record. Distributor: Ladyslipper. Order no.: Indipop 3. $9.95.**
"On this lushly textured, harmonic, innovative album, Sheila Chandra brings together the seeming paradoxes and polarities of her life. Her Indian heritage is steeped in ancient traditions, and she values them, yet feels they must be used in a progressive context.
"The album blends traditional eastern sounds, chants, and instruments (sitar, gamelan, Zildjian cymbals, tabla, tamboura, etc.) with western rhythms and technology to create Indipop. This album is truly one of the most creative and lovely works in our catalog." DIST

Versos de José Martí. **Sara González. 12-inch long-playing record. Distributor: Ladyslipper. Order no.: Nueva Cultura Latinoamericana 0036. $8.95.**
"This Cuban vocalist sings material by José Martí, a Cuban author/journalist/revolutionary who lived in the latter part of the 19th century and was jailed and exiled for his liberation activities." DIST

Village Reflections and Extensions. **Rose Marie Guiraud. 12-inch long-playing record. Distributor: Ladyslipper. Order no.: Makossa 2350. $8.95.**
"'Women of the world, creating a new present and future world, listen

to me: our sun is going to shine' . . . words from her opening song, in the Wobe language, which is native to the Ivory Coast—a republic in West Africa—where Guiraud is from. Others are in French, English, and Appolonian.

"Rose Marie Guiraud is also a choreographer, teacher, dancer, actress (appeared in a docu-drama on women's emancipation which was shown throughout Europe and in 'The Black Medea'), and playwright (her most recent work, 'Mami Wata,' was produced by the La Mama Theater). This incredibly gifted woman explores, interprets and transmits the very basic meanings of African life through her music. Her voice is deep; instrumentation combines African percussion and jazz structures with her original music and lyrics." DIST

We Remember Jean Donovan. Chuck Moore. 1982. 13'. Cassette tape. Distributor: Pacifica Radio Archive. Order no.: KZ1230. $11.

"Jean Donovan was the laywoman killed with three nuns in El Salvador in December 1980. Here her parents, Pat and Ray Donovan, talk about her, the situation in El Salvador now, and recent killings there with Blase Bonpane and David Clennon, an actor in *Missing.*" DIST

Women in Grenada. Sue Supriano and Roxanne Merrifield. 1982. 60'. Cassette tape. Distributor: Pacifica Radio Archive. Order no.: AZ0622. $13.

"The women of Grenada describe their lives under the government of Maurice Bishop, the women's cooperatives, the National Women's Organization, education, health care, sexism, and the role of women in the country." DIST

Women on the Global Assembly Line. Maggie Geddes and Mary Sinclair. 1981. 28'. Cassette tape. Distributor: Pacifica Radio Archive. Order no.: AZ0585. $11.

"When multinational corporations set up factories in Mexico and Hong Kong, they often hire women. Focusing on the electronics industry, this program explores why, and what the conditions are like for the women working on these assembly lines." DIST

Women Unbound: The Role of Women in the People's Republic of China. Helene Rosenbluth and Eloise Klein Healy. 1982. 51'. Cassette tape. Distributor: Pacifica Radio Archive. Order no.: KZ1249.02. $13.

"This program is produced from interviews with women in Shanghai, Nanjing, and Peking. They talk about how the lives of women are changing in modern China. The program is in Mandarin and English." DIST

SUPPLEMENTARY LIST OF AUDIO RESOURCES

Brotando del silencio (Breaking Out of the Silence). Suni Paz. 12-inch long-playing record. Paredon Records. Order no.: 1016. $7.95.

El cancionero popular. Amparo Ochoa. 12-inch long-playing record or cassette tape. Ladyslipper. Order no.: Discos Pueblo 1006 (record), C-1006 (tape). $8.95.

Formando un puente. Sabia. 12-inch long-playing record or cassette tape. Redwood Records. Order no.: 2900.

Sing to Me the Dream. Holly Near and Inti-Illimani. 12-inch long-playing record or cassette tape. Redwood Records. Order no.: 407.

Tiene que ser la luna. Zoriada Santiago. 12-inch long-playing record. Ladyslipper. Order no.: Discos Mila 001. $9.95.

Traditional Women's Music from Ghana. 12-inch long-playing record. Folkways. Order no.: 4257.

Vamos juntos. Amparo Ochoa. 12-inch long-playing record or cassette tape. Ladyslipper. Order no.: Discos Pueblo 1062 (record), C-1062 (tape). $8.95.

INFORMATION SOURCES

For additional information on audio resources related to women in the Third World we suggest that you request catalogs from the distributors listed in this chapter, especially from Ladyslipper and the Pacifica Radio Archive.

In October 1985 the National Federation of Community Broadcasters produced an eight-page listing of programs on community radio stations in the United States that bill themselves as being "by, for, and about women." Single copy: $2.50. The NFCB also publishes a newsletter with descriptions of some of the more than five thousand programs that are available in the NFCB audio library. NFCB, 1314 14 St., NW, Washington, DC 20005.

See the catalogs, directories, and guides described in the books chapter above, as well as these publications from **Third World Resources,** 464 19 St., Oakland, CA 94612:

Asia and Pacific: A Directory of Resources. Compiled and edited by Thomas P. Fenton and Mary J. Heffron. Maryknoll, N.Y., and London: Orbis Books and Zed Books, 1986. 160pp. $9.95, plus $1.50 shipping and handling. Illustrations and indexes.

Latin America and Caribbean: A Directory of Resources. Compiled and edited by Thomas P. Fenton and Mary J. Heffron. Maryknoll, N.Y., and London: Orbis Books and Zed Books, 1986. 160pp. $9.95, plus $1.50 shipping and handling. Illustrations and indexes.

Resource directories on Africa and on the Middle East are forthcoming from Orbis and Zed in 1987.

Third World Resources: A Quarterly Review of Resources from and about the Third World. 4 issues/year. Newsletter. 28cm. 16pp. $25/year (organizational subscription), $25/two years (individual subscription). Inquire for overseas rates. Subscriptions are available on a calendar-year basis only.

Indexes

ORGANIZATIONS

This index contains the names of all organizations associated with the production and/or distribution of resources included in this directory. See the Subjects Index below for references to organizations not directly connected to those resources. Page numbers in bold face signify that the organization's address will be found in the text. If a resource is easily available at a library or bookstore or through some other distributor, the publisher's address is not given.

INDIVIDUALS

This index contains the names of all individuals associated with the production and/or distribution of resources included in this directory.

TITLES

This index contains the names of all the print and audiovisual resources included in this directory. The distributor's address appears either in the text or in the Organizations Index above when we have judged that the resource is not easily available through a library or bookstore.

GEOGRAPHICAL AREAS

This index includes all references to countries and regions mentioned in this resource directory. Names are given as they appear in the resource and imply no political judgment about the legitimacy of national claims. Regional references (e.g., West Africa) are given only when there is a resource that treats the area as a whole. References are provided for organizations in chapter 1 only if they specify a concern for a particular country.

SUBJECTS

This topical index also contains references to organizations not directly related to the production and/or distribution of resources listed in this directory. Keyword descriptions for the issue-focus of organizations in chapter 1 do not appear in this index.

140 INDEXES

DATA
CENTER

Affiliate of the Investigative Resource Center
464 19th St., Oakland, CA 94612 USA (415) 835-4692

The Data Center is an independent, non-profit research and information center. Founded in 1977 the Center provides a range of products and services for the public-interest community on national and international issues of justice and peace.

Custom Research Services

Clipping Service: Data Center staff will monitor and clip any or all of the 400 newspapers and magazines they receive for those who need ongoing information about a given topic, such as human rights in the Philippines.

Search Service: Data Center researchers will search over 400 file drawers of periodical clippings and provide full-text photocopies of articles on corporations, countries, industries, labor issues, and a variety of other political and economic subjects.

Call or write for cost estimates on the Center's custom research services.

Publications

Latin America and Caribbean: The Center produces two regular publications on these regions: *Information Services on Latin America* (monthly) and the *Central America Monitor* (biweekly). Write for a free brochure. The Center has also compiled velo-bound collections of newsclippings on Grenada (1983, 150pp.), Jamaica (1985, 115pp.), and the Sanctuary Movement (1985, 70pp.). $10 each.

Corporate Information Services: The Center publishes two monthly 100-page collections of newspaper and magazine articles on corporate issues: *Corporate Responsibility Monitor* and *Plant Shutdowns Monitor.* Write for subscription rates. Data Center *Corporate Profiles* are custom-designed collections of articles from the media and of government and corporate documents on any of 5,000 U.S. and foreign corporations. Write for rates.

The Data Center also publishes well-organized and up-to-date collections of newsclippings on the political and religious right, terrorism, U.S. foreign policy, and environmental pollution.

The Data Center is a member-supported organization. Write for a schedule of fees and a list of benefits. Contributions are tax-deductible.

Third World Resources

464 19th Street   Oakland, CA 94612

Third World Resources gathers, catalogs, annotates, and publicizes education and action resources from and about the Third World.

Resource Directories

Twelve directories are being compiled on these subjects:

Third World general	Food, hunger, agribusiness
Africa	Human rights
Asia & Pacific	Militarism, peace, disarmament
Latin America & Caribbean	Native peoples & natural resources
Middle East	Nuclear arms & energy
Women in the Third World	TNCs & labor

Quarterly Newsletter

The *Third World Resources* newsletter contains notices and descriptive listings of organizations and newly released print, audiovisual, and other educational resources on Third World regions and issues. Inquire for subscription rates. Sample copy: US $1.

Each 16-page issue contains a unique 4-page insert with a comprehensive listing of resources on one particular region or subject. Inquire about discounts for bulk purchases.

Documentation Center

All resources are cataloged and integrated into the library collection of the Data Center where they are accessible to Center library users and Search Service clients. Bibliographical data are stored in a computerized data base to facilitate identification and retrieval of cross-referenced resources.

Third World Resources is a financially independent project of the Data Center, a non-profit, tax-exempt (501.c.3) resource center. Contributions to Third World Resources are tax-deductible.

THIRD WORLD RESOURCES

**A QUARTERLY REVIEW OF RESOURCES
FROM & ABOUT THE THIRD WORLD**

Keep the invaluable information in this resource directory complete, correct, and up-to-date by subscribing to *Third World Resources* (ISSN 8755-8831).

Third World Resources provides descriptions and capsule reviews of organizations, books, periodicals, pamphlets, audiovisual, and other education and action resources on Third World regions and issues. Entries include complete ordering information and are indexed annually. The Editors' Notes column contains updates and corrections of information published in each of the resource directories in the 12-volume set.

Each issue of the 16-page newsletter contains a unique 4-page pullout with comprehensive listings of resources on one Third World region or issue. Available at bulk discounts, these 4-page guides are excellent inexpensive handouts for talks, workshops, and study programs.

THIRD WORLD RESOURCES

**A QUARTERLY REVIEW OF RESOURCES
FROM & ABOUT THE THIRD WORLD**

Keep the invaluable information in this resource directory complete, correct, and up-to-date by subscribing to *Third World Resources* (ISSN 8755-8831).

Third World Resources provides descriptions and capsule reviews of organizations, books, periodicals, pamphlets, audiovisual, and other education and action resources on Third World regions and issues. Entries include complete ordering information and are indexed annually. The Editors' Notes column contains updates and corrections of information published in each of the resource directories in the 12-volume set.

Each issue of the 16-page newsletter contains a unique 4-page pullout with comprehensive listings of resources on one Third World region or issue. Available at bulk discounts, these 4-page guides are excellent inexpensive handouts for talks, workshops, and study programs.

ORDER FORM

Newsletter Subscription Form

☐ Please enter my subscription to Third World Resources at this rate:
   U.S. and Canada: ___ Organizational ($25/year) or ___ Individual ($25/two years)
   Foreign Airmail: ___ Organizational ($35/year) or ___ Individual ($40/two years)
   Note: Subscriptions run on a calendar-year basis only. Individual subscribers will receive
   a prorated refund if they decide to cancel at the end of the first year.

☐ Please send a sample copy of *Third World Resources* ($2).

Third World Resource Directory

☐ Please send _____ copy/copies of the *Third World Resource Directory: A Guide to
   Organizations and Publications.* Compiled and edited by Thomas P. Fenton and Mary
   J. Heffron. Maryknoll, N.Y.: Orbis Books, 1984, 304pp. $17.95. Add (per copy): $1.50
   for postage in North America; $2.50 for book rate postage overseas; $6 for airmail
   overseas.

☐ Enclosed is information on our organization for inclusion in future resource directories
   or the *Third World Resources* newsletter.

☐ Please add my/our name to your mailing list.

NAME _____

ADDRESS _____

_____

_____

Enclosed is US$ _____ for the materials I/we ordered above. Please make check/
money order payable in U.S. dollars to **Third World Resources** and send to 464 19th Street,
Oakland, CA 94612 USA.

ORDER FORM

Newsletter Subscription Form

☐ Please enter my subscription to Third World Resources at this rate:
   U.S. and Canada: ___ Organizational ($25/year) or ___ Individual ($25/two years)
   Foreign Airmail: ___ Organizational ($35/year) or ___ Individual ($40/two years)
   Note: Subscriptions run on a calendar-year basis only. Individual subscribers will receive
   a prorated refund if they decide to cancel at the end of the first year.

☐ Please send a sample copy of *Third World Resources* ($2).

Third World Resource Directory

☐ Please send _____ copy/copies of the *Third World Resource Directory: A Guide to
   Organizations and Publications.* Compiled and edited by Thomas P. Fenton and Mary
   J. Heffron. Maryknoll, N.Y.: Orbis Books, 1984, 304pp. $17.95. Add (per copy): $1.50
   for postage in North America; $2.50 for book rate postage overseas; $6 for airmail
   overseas.

☐ Enclosed is information on our organization for inclusion in future resource directories
   or the *Third World Resources* newsletter.

☐ Please add my/our name to your mailing list.

NAME _____

ADDRESS _____

_____

_____

Enclosed is US$ _____ for the materials I/we ordered above. Please make check/
money order payable in U.S. dollars to **Third World Resources** and send to 464 19th Street,
Oakland, CA 94612 USA.